PLAIN
TALK
ON
Galatians

BOOKS BY DR. GUTZKE . . .

PLAIN
TALK
ON
Galatians

MANFORD GEORGE GUTZKE
PH. D.

ZONDERVAN
PUBLISHING HOUSE OF THE ZONDERVAN CORPORATION
GRAND RAPIDS, MICHIGAN 49506

Copyright © 1972 by
Baker Book House Co.

Copyright transferred to The Zondervan Corporation, 1978.

Library of Congress Catalog Card No: 72-90329

ISBN 0-310-25651-8

Printed in the United States of America

83   84   85   86   87   88 — 10   9   8   7   6   5   4   3

CONTENTS

PART ONE

INTRODUCTION

1

THE MEANING
OF A NEW TESTAMENT EPISTLE

If a person is already a Christian, why should he listen to preaching?

The Epistle of Paul to the Galatians is simply a letter from Paul to believers in the community called Galatia. This was an area in Asia Minor. The people were Greek, they spoke Greek, and they were called Galatians. The full meaning of this is obvious; there is nothing obscure about the circumstances. It is as if a letter was sent to the Christians who live in your home state.

In studying any New Testament epistle we need to ask, To whom was the letter written? In this case Paul was writing to believers. To whom is this letter to go? Paul says it is to the churches of Galatia. Notice that the word *churches* is plural, with a small *c*. They did not have denominations then, but they did have individual congregations. Now we all understand, I expect, that there is the Bible doctrine of the Church. We think of God the Father, and God the Son, and God the Holy Spirit; and we think of the Church, the body of Christ. Usually when we speak of the Church as the body of Christ, we refer to it with a capital *C*, because we are thinking of all Christians as being the one Church which is the body of Christ.

When we speak of churches, we mean congregations. This use of the word occurs in the New Testament when one writer indicates, "to the church which is in thy house" (Philem. 1:2). When we use the word *church* in the sense of congregation, we generally use a small *c*; and in this letter such use referred to the groups of believers that were found in this general area of Galatia. The *churches* were groups composed of individuals who had accepted Christ Jesus.

It is important to notice that this letter was not written "to all the well-meaning people in Galatia." "Well-meaning" would not be good enough. Neither was the letter sent "to all the good people in Galatia" for the same reason. Nor is the letter addressed "to all those who are working to go to heaven." No, Christians are not working to go to heaven: Christians are going to heaven by the grace of God. They are expecting to go to heaven because they believe in the Lord Jesus Christ.

Finally, this letter was not written to all the people who live in Galatia. It was written to the churches of Galatia; that is, to those who know that they are sinners, and have believed Jesus Christ died for them. They have trusted in the Lord Jesus Christ and received Him as their Savior. They understand now that they belong to God. Because they now have the Holy Spirit within them, they want the name of the Lord Jesus Christ to be magnified and glorified. That is pretty much what is meant when we speak of a Christian and that is what we mean by the Church. This letter was written to "such as believe in Christ" and was sent to the churches of Galatia.

At the same time this message is a timeless one to Christians anywhere in the world. It is true that this was written in Paul's lifetime and therefore belongs to the early days of the church, but the message is true for all times. Study in this Epistle to the Galatians will reveal that nothing local, nothing immediate, nothing temporal, is referred to. What is revealed is true anytime, anywhere, every place.

This is a letter, and a letter is used for conveying ideas from one person to another. This is just that. Paul wrote this letter to the believers in Galatia to show them the true, original meaning of the gospel. Paul, who understood the gospel, wrote to these young Galatian Christians who seemed to have gotten some wrong ideas. He discusses with them the meaning of the gospel, that he might help to straighten out some of the wrong ideas they had.

Someone might ask, "Why write to them? Were they not already believers?" It is true they were already believers, but they would need spiritual food to live and grow. Just because a person is alive, does not mean he now stops eating. Anyone would know he eats to live. Exactly! And that's why Christian people read the Bible. It is true that reading the Bible and listening to the message of the Bible is what produced them as Christians, but "now as newborn babes they desire the sincere milk of the word that they may grow thereby." So any time that anybody asks, "Why should any person want to be reading the Bible?" say, "Because he needs its nourishment." They may say, "Well, has not that person already read the Bible?" Yes, even though I ate yesterday and the day before, I need food again today to live. Just so I need to feed on God's Holy Word for my spirit's sake. That is the reason why Christians read and study Scripture over and over again.

What then is in this material that is called the Epistle to the Galatians? What is in this discussion that will show the true, original meaning of the gospel? This Scripture will show that Jesus Christ is now alive in heaven, able and competent to completely deliver anybody putting his trust in Him. The whole discussion will deal with living a life of victory and triumph by the help of the living God through the Lord Jesus Christ who is in the presence of God, made available to and operative in us by the Holy Spirit. In this epistle, you will find no argument to prove that God is real. The Christians know God is real, but face practical questions: God being real, how should a Christian relate himself to God? How does God work in a believer? And then again, this epistle has nothing in it to prove that the gospel is true. The Galatians knew the gospel was true. There was no use of going over that ground again; they understood it very well.

The Christian believes in the Lord Jesus Christ. But where did he hear about Him? He found out about the Lord Jesus Christ in Scripture. When he discovered the promises of God in Scripture and believed those promises, they became operative in his life, so that he was blessed by them. To argue with a Christian that the Bible is true is as if someone came to me and argued with me that water is wet. I know it's wet—I drink it! So far as the believer is concerned, he believes the Bible. No preaching is needed to arouse acceptance. Paul is not trying to tell these people, "Be sure to believe." They are already believers.

However, there is in this letter some warning about "other gospels." The fact is that it is possible for well-meaning Christians to get off on the wrong foot in their thinking. Errors will be straightened out by understanding the true gospel. Paul will reason with these people to show the true meaning of the gospel that they have already received, the believing of which has given them peace with God through the Lord Jesus Christ and the indwelling of the Holy Spirit.

PART TWO

THE GOSPEL
MUST NOT BE
COMPROMISED

(1:1-19)

2

SALUTATION
(1:1-5)

Have you ever been sent as an agent?

> Paul, an apostle, (not of men, neither by man, but by Jesus
> Christ, and God the Father, who raised him from the dead;)
> And all the brethren which are with me, unto the churches
> of Galatia: Grace be to you and peace from God the
> Father, and from our Lord Jesus Christ.—1:1-3

This opening sentence simply says, "Paul and all the brethren
which are with me, unto the churches of Galatia: Grace be to you
and peace." This is Paul's characteristic salutation, the way he opens
his letters. It is very much the way a person would say, "My dear
friend." But there is a great deal packed into these few words. Paul
draws attention to the function he has been given to perform as an
apostle. It is in this responsibility that he is writing. He has nothing
to say about himself as a man, his education, his personal understanding of human nature or the affairs of history that might qualify
him to speak.

Paul starts by introducing himself: "Paul, an apostle"—just that.
An apostle is a person who has been sent to represent—sent to
perform something in the name of the person that sent him. This is
the one thing that Paul was: a sent man. He is writing this letter
because he had a mission to perform as one who had been sent by
God to do something. The one thing the Galatian Christians were to

understand was that he was writing as a personally sent, accredited representative of God; and he was going to write that way.

Paul emphasizes his authority when he writes, "not of men." He wants it understood he is not functioning as an apostle because human beings asked him to perform this service. There may be those who are preaching because they feel that their community, the society they are in, has produced in them the desire to help others; and so they are doing what they can in this way. But this was not the case with Paul. His call was not of men. Men did not send him and men did not show him what to say. "Neither by man"—he was not authorized by man—"but by Jesus Christ." He had been authorized by Christ Jesus, and "God the Father who raised him from the dead." Later Paul will bring these two Persons together—Jesus Christ and God the Father; but here at the outset he points out that he was given his apostleship, his authority, from these two.

While Paul takes full responsibility for what he is going to write, this was a letter that would have been agreed to by all the other workers who were with Paul. "All the brethren which are with me, unto the churches of Galatia"—the groups of Christian people who are in Galatia. Many of the epistles of the New Testament are written to churches; that is to say, to Christians in communion with each other. Among the letters of Paul recorded in the New Testament were some that he wrote to individuals. He wrote to Timothy and to Titus, who were preachers; he also wrote to an individual when he wrote to Philemon. But most of the epistles of Paul, as well as the writings of James and of Peter, are written to groups, that is, to churches.

"Grace be to you and peace from God the Father, and from our Lord Jesus Christ." In this statement are "grace" and "peace," two great words: so easy to say, but with such profound meaning. "Grace be to you" is Paul's prayer. "May you have grace: may God give you grace." Grace comes from God. Grace is something God gives which somehow enters into a person to enable him to do the will of God. When grace comes to a Christian it opens his heart, giving him the inward disposition and moving his will to give inward strength to obey. The Christian will find himself moved to obey the will of God by grace. Grace is never given to anyone only to make him happy and glad in himself. It is given so that a believer may respond to God as he should. When the believer comes to know God's Word, often he is afflicted with the realization that in himself he just would not follow its principles. Sometimes he does not want to obey; and sometimes even if he wanted to, he could not do it.

The apostle Paul wrote: "What I want to do I don't do, and what I don't want to do, that's what I do." Thus he goes on to say in the seventh chapter of Romans: "If then I do that which I would not, it is no longer I that do it, but sin that dwelleth in me." Now just the way sin in a human being can prompt him to disobey God, so grace operates in a Christian to move him to do the will of God. Sin is in man simply because he is a human being, a child of Adam: he is sinful by nature. But God will in response to faith exercise His grace in the heart, so that the believer will from within want to obey God. As sin will cause a man to disobey God, so grace will prompt a Christian to obey God. It is marvelous to remember that "where sin abounds, grace does much more abound." There is always this big difference between sin and grace, so that if a person has grace in his heart it can be said of him: "Greater is he that is in you, than he that is in the world" (I John 4:4).

When Paul is saying to the Galatian church, "May you have the grace of God," he means, "May you have help from God to obey Him." "And peace be unto you." Peace is something a person experiences. It is something inside the heart. Grace is something given to you, operative in you; and grace gives strength to perform. A person does things by the grace of God which is in the heart, moving him to want to obey God and enabling him to do it. Peace is something a person has, something that has been given to him. Paul writes in the Philippian Letter "that the peace of God which passeth all understanding shall guard your hearts and minds in Christ Jesus." Peace is an inward feeling, a sense that everything is as it should be. Peace does not mean the cessation of all activity. It does not mean total silence. It does not mean total deadness—to be completely without any emotion at all. Peace is a matter of harmony; it is when everything is in its place; it is when everything is as it should be, running smoothly.

"Who gave himself for our sins, that he might deliver us from this present evil world, according to the will of God and our Father: To whom be glory for ever and ever. Amen" (1:4, 5). In these words to the Galatians is the answer to the question: Why did Jesus of Nazareth go to Calvary? Here it is: "who gave himself for our sins, that he might deliver us from this present evil world." This is the heart of the gospel of the Lord Jesus Christ. This is the particular truth which Christians tell the world. Too often people think Christians are telling them they ought to do good and be good. People in the world seem to expect the church to be preaching at them, that they should be doing better than they are doing. They should be nicer, sweeter people. They should all live together happily and improve things around them. Of course none of that is bad, but that is truly not the gospel of the Lord Jesus Christ.

The Christian gospel is about Jesus Christ. He came to give Himself for our sins, for the purpose "that he might deliver us from this present evil world." This is the thread Paul weaves throughout this whole Epistle to the Galatians. In this verse is the insight to everything Paul will be talking about. Throughout this epistle, the one truth he will press home is that Jesus Christ has done in Himself what it takes to deliver men from this present evil world. To say "who gave himself for our sin" means He offered Himself up to die in order that men may be delivered "from this present evil world." "This present evil world" refers to the personal predicament every Christian faces in his everyday affairs. To know what is meant by "the world" one should read I John 2:16: "The lust of the flesh, the lust of the eye, and the pride of life"; these things are "of the world." In other words, all that is made up of appetite and imagination and vanity, the things that please self, when taken together make up "the world" as referred to in the New Testament. Why do people do what they are doing, running to and fro? They are seeking what they like and what pleases them. Man follows what he wants, rather than what God wants; and in the sight of God this is evil.

"This present world," the one in which the Christian lives, is in itself evil. <u>Its influence will cause the Christian</u> to be more vain, more proud, more selfish than he would be. The Lord Jesus came to deliver His own from this influence: "that he might deliver us from this present evil world." This is the wonderful story. He Himself voluntarily came into this world: was born in this world and lived in this world, yet without sin. Living in this world, He showed His own people how to do it acceptably to God. Strange as it may seem, the secret of this is that the believer must die! He must die to self, to the things of this world. That is the only way to live here pleasing to God. The Christian takes himself, his flesh, to the cross; this sets him free from the world. The believer reckons himself indeed to be dead in the flesh and alive in the spirit; because when a person dies in his human nature the temptations of the world will not appeal to him any longer.

Things that look so nice do not mean a thing to a corpse; things that feel so nice do not attract a dead man; things that a person would be pleased to eat or to drink would not mean much if that person would reckon himself dead. This great gospel truth is that Christians are set free in the death of the Lord Jesus Christ because they are not any longer in bondage to the flesh, which is so beset by temptations on all sides to sin.

If a person would fall into a river, so far as he is concerned, that water is "evil": it will drown him. How would he be "set free" from that water? Would he not be set free from that water and its dangers by being delivered out of it? If someone would come and lift him out of the river, would he not be delivered? How would you "deliver" a child from a burning house? Would you do it by putting the fire out? Or would you do it by getting the child out of the house?

This is what the Lord Jesus Christ did when He came into this world. He did not come into this world to improve the world so that subsequent generations, thousands of years afterward, would be able to live in peace. <u>He came to "deliver us from this present evil world"</u> that we are in now. It is actually distressing to hear preaching and teaching that seems to be saying that if all men would do like this or that, then in two, three, four generations—that is, in a hundred, a hundred and fifty, two hundred years—everything would be nice and lovely. The Christian gospel does not tell men to wait until the world clears up, but to get the man out of the world.

"Who will deliver us from this present evil world, according to the will of God and our Father" has always been the purpose of God. When Paul writes, "To whom be glory for ever and ever," he prays that God's plan may bear fruit in the saving of souls through Christ Jesus. So here at the beginning of Galatians, in verses 4 and 5, is to be found the very heart of the whole Christian gospel and of the whole Bible, that Jesus Christ "gave himself for our sins, that he might deliver us from this present evil world." He came to get believers out of it, "according to the will of God and our Father."

3

THE TRUTH MUST
NOT BE TWISTED
(1:6-9)

Do you know how Paul would have acted?

When Paul writes: "I marvel that ye are so soon removed from him that called you into the grace of Christ unto another gospel" he means to say, "I am surprised that you have been so easily changed over from the one who preached to you and called you into the grace of Christ, to another gospel. You've listened to somebody else." This is the plain way the apostle expresses himself:

> I marvel that ye are so soon removed from him that called you into the grace of Christ unto another gospel: Which is not another; but there be some that trouble you, and would pervert the gospel of Christ. But though we, or an angel from heaven, preach any other gospel unto you than that

which we have preached unto you, let him be accursed. As we said before, so say I now again, If any man preach any other gospel unto you than that ye have received, let him be accursed.—1:6-9

The word "gospel" means "good news." Paul writes, "I marvel that ye are so soon removed from him that called you into the grace of Christ." That was the kind of preaching that had saved these people: they had been "called into the grace of Christ." So often today public preaching seems to be a case of sending people out to do something. Sometimes it is the kind of preaching that amounts to talking about things: explaining things and arguing about things. But Paul called men "into the grace of Christ." This meant giving them the invitation: calling them into such a relationship with Christ that He would work in them by His grace, delivering them from this present evil world. The Galatians had had such a preacher, who called his hearers "into the grace of Christ," calling them into trusting in Christ, calling them into believing in Christ, so that Christ could operate in them by His grace.

"I am surprised that you are so soon removed from the one who called you into the grace of Christ unto another gospel." When Paul refers to what they had heard as "another gospel" he is quick to point out "which is not another." Paul means that the teaching they have been hearing is not a real gospel; it is not good news. "But there be some that trouble you, and would pervert the gospel of Christ." There were preachers among them that would take the things Paul had preached in the name of the Lord Jesus Christ and twist them. "Pervert" is to "twist," to make it different. This means these others were preaching the facts about Christ in some other way than the way in which Paul had preached.

By way of an illustration, consider what happens when a young couple is going to get married. Is it not true that when they set up housekeeping, the young man will have someone to look after the house? Would he not expect that she would prepare his meals? Is it not quite possible that she will wash his clothes, will clean up his room, make his bed, and do such things for him? This would follow their getting married. But if that young man started thinking about getting married so that he would have free laundry, a free cook and maid, he would be perverting the idea of getting married. In just this way it is possible to pervert the gospel of Christ, and this had been done in Galatia after Paul had been there as a missionary.

"But though we, or an angel from heaven, preach any other gospel unto you than that which we have preached unto you, let him be accursed" (1:8). Paul had preached the truth when he called the Galatians into the grace of the Lord Jesus Christ. Any other kind of message is not the truth; and anybody who preaches any other kind of message should be shut out, should be put away. This word "accursed" does not particularly refer to ill-tempered profanity. It actually means "let him be put away from you," "let him be out from among you." "Repudiate that person" is the main idea here. When Paul writes, "Though we, or an angel from heaven, preach any other gospel unto you than that which we have preached," he indicates what he thought of the preaching he had done. He had called them into the grace of Christ, which was the truth; and nothing else but that is the truth. Souls are saved in and through the Lord Jesus Christ and not by any other method. This is what Paul had preached, and this is what he was going to stand by.

"As we said before, so say I now again, If any man preach any other gospel unto you than that ye have received, let him be accursed" (1:9). Paul was not pressing them to hold fast what they had received merely because it came first; that was not the idea. The gospel they had received was the truth. The truth is that Jesus Christ died for our sins, and we are saved in Him; anything else is not the truth. That is all there is to say about it. Anything different from this ought not to be preached in the name of the Lord Jesus Christ. The way in which Paul is restating his judgment makes it pretty clear that this was not a case of bad temper.

If it should be said, "Oh, well, Paul just got mad; and when Paul got mad, he said if anybody didn't agree with me, let him be put out." This is not the way it was. Paul wrote, "As we said before, so say I now again." Paul was deliberate about this matter. "If any man preach any other gospel unto you than that ye have received"—than the one Paul had preached to them—"let him be accursed." Put him away! So far as Paul is concerned, he reveals plainly that a pastor is concerned that his people get the truth. Any other message than the truth is not acceptable, and the man who preaches any other message than the true message is not acceptable.

4

NOT HUMAN
IN ORIGIN
(1:10-19)

Do you realize that the apostles did not invent this message?

In Galatians 1:10-19 the apostle Paul writes about himself and about his preaching. He raises the question: "For do I now persuade men, or God?" Which is a way of saying, "Am I now seeking to be acceptable in the sight of men or seeking to be acceptable in the sight of God?" "Or do I seek to please men? for if I yet pleased men, I should not be the servant of Christ." Paul points out that if he were saying the things he thought men would want to hear, he would not qualify as a servant of Christ.

"But I certify you, brethren, that the gospel which was preached of me is not after man" (1:11). Paul emphasized that when he was preaching the gospel among them, the message he brought was not the kind of message that human beings would organize and bring. When anyone gets up to talk he is sure ·to have ideas; and the question for the listener is, Where did he get his ideas? Sometimes a man gets ideas out of his own heart; sometimes he gets an idea out of what he reads; and sometimes he gets an idea out of the revelation from God through His Word. When Paul said, "I certify you, brethren, that the gospel which was preached of me is not after man," he meant he did not get it from any human source. Then he explains what he means: "For I neither received it of man, neither was I taught it, but by the revelation of Jesus Christ" (1:12). Paul did not get what he was preaching by watching people, nor by listening to people; he got what he was saying "by the revelation of Jesus Christ." He means that he actually saw in Jesus Christ the truth he was sharing with the Galatians as he preached.

Then Paul goes on to say more about himself: "For ye have heard of my conversation in time past in the Jews' religion [the word "conversation" means "manner of life"], how that beyond measure I persecuted the church of God, and wasted it" (1:13). When he says "beyond measure" he means "beyond all reason"; he was unreasonable in the things he did. "I persecuted the church of God [the believers] and wasted it"; that is, he despoiled it, he scattered it, he worked to diminish it. "And profited in the Jews' religion above many my equals in mine own nation, being more exceedingly zealous of the traditions of my fathers" (1:14). Yet this zealous Pharisee had a clear conscience at the time about his activities. He tried in every way possible to exterminate the church. He was what could be called a zealous, eager, anxious, dedicated Jew. And, of course, he was wrong. Just being sincere isn't enough. A person can be dedicated to his purpose and be entirely wrong, simply because he can be dedicated to something that is of his own mind.

Paul explains why he knows the gospel was not out of his own mind:

> For ye have heard of my conversation [manner of life] in time past in the Jews' religion, how that beyond measure I persecuted the church of God [the people who believed in Jesus Christ], and wasted it [I scattered it, I abused it in every way I possibly could]; And profited in the Jews' religion [I put myself out to grow in it] above many my equals [people of my own age] in mine own nation, being more exceedingly zealous of the traditions of my fathers. But when it pleased God, who separated me from my mother's womb, and called me by his grace, To reveal his Son in me, that I might preach him among the heathen;

immediately I conferred not with flesh and blood.—1:13-16

This shows that Paul even as a Pharisee certainly believed in God. "And separated me from my mother's womb." God made him and gave him life. In thinking about God, Paul always kept in mind he was dealing with his creator, who gave him life "and called me by his grace." Paul knew he was created, made by God, and that he was called to trust in God: called to give himself over to God, "by God's grace." Paul understood it pleased God to reveal the truth to him that Jesus Christ in living was in the very person of Paul. This is vital. It was not only that he heard the right thing about Jesus Christ, but also God enabled him inwardly to see the truth. He realized it was the work of God to "reveal his Son in me, that I might preach him among the heathen." This is revealed throughout Scripture. God gives blessing in order that His servant may be a blessing to others. God reveals truth to His own in order that they may share this with others.

Paul understood this was what God was doing with him: "To reveal his Son in me, that I might preach him among the heathen; immediately I conferred not with flesh and blood" (1:16). When Paul had this spiritual experience of being called by the Lord, he did not run immediately to other Christians to find out what they thought about it. "Neither went I up to Jerusalem to them which were apostles before me; but I went into Arabia, and returned again unto Damascus" (1:17). He was preaching and teaching all the time he was there; but he did not get in touch with the main church, so he could not have learned his message from them. "Then after three years I went up to Jerusalem to see Peter, and abode with him fifteen days. But other of the apostles saw I none, save James the Lord's brother" (1:18-19). In this way, Paul is saying, it would have been impossible for him to find out from men what he ought to preach. He did not get to know the older Christians well enough. Paul knew the facts of the life of Christ. He may well have known the facts of the earthly life of the Lord Jesus Christ before he even met Him on the Damascus road. But the meaning of those facts came to him directly from the Lord in heaven. There need be no question as to what Paul thought about the message he was to preach; it was not human in origin.

Paul said bluntly that he was not seeking to please men, and he had an adequate reason for this. Because he had been reconciled to God, and had been called of God, he wanted the favor of God. He did not care about the favor of men. The message he had to deliver was not something he had seen, nor something he had reasoned out. Paul did not analyze the human situation, and arrive at the conclusion that the gospel would be a good thing. He makes it clearly obvious that he had not been helped to this frame of mind: "for I neither received it of man, nor was taught it, but by the revelation of Jesus Christ." The Lord Himself showed Paul the truth about God's plan through His Son. The Damascus road experience for Paul started something that was not only valid, but also it was for eternity.

PART THREE

THERE IS
ONLY ONE GOSPEL

(1:20—2:14)

5

THE GOSPEL MATTERS, NOT THE PREACHER
(1:20–2:2)

Do you realize that it is the gospel that matters, and not the preacher?

The gospel—that believers should be delivered from this present evil world—is not any man's personal idea. In the Book of Galatians the apostle Paul describes the gospel in this way, saying that Christ Jesus gave Himself for sins so that believers in Him would be delivered from this present evil world. That truth is not man's idea, but God's. Credit is often given to preachers personally. For example, when a preacher is reputed to be effective and powerful so that his church has been built up, it is common practice to give credit to the preacher. Men praise him. If, on the other hand, people do not seem to respond to his preaching, it is the usual thing to blame the preacher. After all, isn't it the preacher that matters? In just this way men often look to preachers to help them solve their problems. Men want the preacher to tell them what to do; then, if it turns out well, he is a good preacher. But is this the right way? Is this, after all, what the preacher is supposed to be doing? According to the Book of Galatians the gospel is based on the plan of God. This is something God has in mind to do.

John 3:16 is the very heart of the gospel: "For God so loved the world that he gave his only begotten Son, that whosoever believeth in him should not perish, but have everlasting life." This is salvation, and the way of salvation is God's idea. It is not dependent on human beings, nor is it dependent on any preacher, smart or good as he may be. It is God's idea.

When Paul preached there was no question in his mind but that there is only one way to be saved. It is not any way, it is not many ways, there is but one way to be saved. The Lord Jesus Himself said, "I am the door"—*the* door. He didn't say, "I am *a* door"; He said, "I am *the* door, by me if any man enter in he shall be saved." In fact, He went on to say that if anybody tries to enter in any other way, he is a thief and a robber. And again the Lord Jesus said to His disciples, "I am the way, the truth, and the life. No man cometh to the Father but by me." Speaking before the council, the apostle Peter said, "There is none other name under heaven given among men, whereby we must be saved" (Acts 4:12).

Salvation is only through the Lord Jesus Christ. "He that hath the Son hath life; and he that hath not the Son of God hath not life" (I John 5:12). The way of Jesus Christ is eternal. It was in God's mind from the beginning. Christ Jesus was the Lamb slain before the foundation of the world. It has always been in God's mind, and it will be in God's mind until the very end of time. This was God's original plan, that He would save to "the uttermost" those who would come to Him through the Lord Jesus Christ, because the Lord Jesus Christ would forever be alive to bring them to God and to pray for them. This is God's way, and in Hebrews 13:8 it is written: "Jesus Christ the same yesterday, and today, and for ever."

It is important to realize this because this was Paul's problem. The Galatians had heard another gospel. Paul was firm in what he had to say to them. There was no other gospel; there was no other way. This was not because he thought of it, and not because he was smart or good. This is the truth as it is in Jesus Christ, and Paul presents this truth. As to any other message, Paul does not hesitate in his judgment: the others are wrong. "Though we, or an angel . . . preach any other gospel unto you, . . . let him be accursed" (1:8). He goes on to say, "As we said before, so say I now again, If any man preach any other gospel unto you than that ye have received, let him be accursed" (1:9).

This is a positive, straightforward statement; and it is clear. There can be no question about this. Paul's argument as to its authenticity is to be found in Galatians 1:20—2:2. He is arguing for the truth that the gospel message which he was preaching was from God, by saying that he obviously did not get his ideas from men since he had so little to do with the early Christians. Paul met the Lord Jesus Christ on the Damascus road. The Lord dealt with him personally. Paul continues his argument with these words:

> Now the things which I write unto you, behold, before God, I lie not. Afterwards I came into the regions of Syria and Cilicia; And was unknown by face unto the churches of Judaea which were in Christ: But they had heard only, That he which persecuted us in times past now preacheth the faith which once he destroyed. (1:20-23)

The churches in Judea did not know him personally, since they had never seen him face to face. But they knew of his witness; and the report that they heard was that whereas once upon a time he was opposed to Christ, now he was preaching Christ. This went on for fourteen years. Paul preached the gospel of the Lord Jesus Christ as an evangelist, as a missionary, and as an apostle. With Scripture in hand and the Holy Spirit in his heart, Paul had personal dealings with the Lord Jesus Christ; and he preached this message to everyone. This message he preached was from God.

"Then fourteen years after I went up again to Jerusalem with Barnabas, and took Titus with me also" (2:1). He went to Jerusalem to discuss something that had to do with the Greeks and with bringing Gentiles into the Christian Church. He went with Barnabas, who had been his companion in preaching, and Titus, who was one of his converts and who had become a great preacher himself. When he wrote "And I went up by revelation" he means to say "by the guidance of God." Paul did not plan this. The Lord led him to Jerusalem; so to Jerusalem he went.

"And I went up by revelation, and communicated unto them that gospel which I preach among the Gentiles, but privately to them which were of reputation, lest by any means I should run, or had run, in vain" (2:2). When Paul went up to Jerusalem he had a private

conference with responsible people, so that the trip would be worth-while. There is something to be learned here about human nature. If something is discussed in public so that everyone talks about it, it can waste away. Paul wanted to be sure that would not happen with the gospel; so when he came to Jerusalem he met with a few responsible people to discuss with them the gospel he had been preaching. He went because he was led to go; he shared the message which he preached privately with responsible persons, so that his mission would not be in vain. He made no attempt to overrule or overwhelm anyone. He wanted to find out what God had in mind. Paul chose this way of showing that the gospel he was preaching was not his own. He was emphasizing the fact that it is not the preacher that counts: it is the gospel that counts.

6

CONTENTION MAY
BE UNAVOIDABLE
(2:3-5)

Do you realize that there may be persons in the congregation whose ideas should be challenged?

The truth of the gospel may need to be defended within the church itself, right among the members of a congregation. There are popular ideas that can be misleading. For instance, it is a common thing to say "one man is as good as another." This simply is not true, and everyone knows it quite well. People would not elect just any man to any office. In hiring people, men do not hire just anyone. The truth of the matter is, one man is not as good as another.

There is a democratic tradition which can enter into the mind. It is customary to say that "All men are born equal." To say, "All men are equal," is to say, "All men are the same size"—that all men are the same height, that all men have the same weight. Now it is true that all men are counted as equal in the matter of opportunity. It is the democratic way to say that each man should get his turn. Every man should have his opportunity to do the most that he can do. Certainly! But when it comes to competence, to ability, of course men are not equal. There are strong people and there are weak people. This creates a problem for Christians to face, and so they say that "the strong should bear the infirmities of the weak and not to please themselves."

Another popular idea that can mislead is this, "Each man has a right to his own opinion." When that is said, one should not imply that one man's opinion is as right as another man's opinion. That doesn't follow. Some men are wrong; some men make mistakes.

It is often said, "What a person thinks is right, is right for him." This is not true! Some people will take poison when they think they are taking food. Their thinking that it is food does not make it so. It is what it is, whether right or wrong; and that person could be wrong. Actually this is why some people die from accidents: they thought wrong.

Again man will say, "He has as much right to state his views as anyone else." This is actually a very questionable thing. What are his views? They could be in error; and when error is stated and tolerated as truth, it can win acceptance to the hurt of the people. A man can make up a story that sounds a whole lot nicer than the truth does. Truth sometimes is hard! In society today there are Pure Food and Drug Laws. They are valid and intelligent. Any container of food sold in the public market must have listed on the label the ingredients in it. This is all done to avoid making a mistake.

This is important for Christian education today. Caution! Teachers should be careful in matters of gospel teaching. It is popular today to say that there should be no controversy. People do not want prolonged discussion or argument. There must be no questioning of the other's views. Anything he says sincerely he should be allowed to say. If the teacher brings out new and different ideas, people tend to think he is brilliant because he is different from the others.

Paul took his responsibility seriously to judge the doctrine of any man who would preach. Paul shows he would not by any means go along with the popular notion that one man's ideas are as good as another man's ideas. Listen to what Paul has to say:

> But neither Titus, who was with me, being a Greek, was compelled to be circumcised: And that because of false brethren unawares brought in, who came in privily to spy out our liberty which we have in Christ Jesus, that they might bring us into bondage: To whom we gave place by subjection, no, not for an hour; that the truth of the gospel might continue with you.—2:3-5

The question confronting the church was whether the Gentiles in becoming Christians should first become Jews. It was a Jewish custom that when a man became a Jew, he submitted to the ceremony of circumcision, which was a mark of the covenant that had been given to Abraham. There were those in the church at Ephesus who claimed that if a person was going to be a real Christian, he should first of all be thus marked like a Jew. Paul pointed out that God had seen fit to bless Gentiles who did not have this ceremonial marking on them. This had been a big controversy in the church at large; and Paul, Barnabas, and Titus had gone to Jerusalem to meet with the elders of the church there to discuss this whole matter. Paul came with Barnabas who was his companion, and he brought Titus who was a Greek; but he would not let them circumcise Titus.

It is written (Acts 16:3) that when Paul took Timothy to be with him, he had him circumcised. But Timothy's mother was a Jewess; so it was proper for Timothy to be circumcised, since he was in part Jewish and thus would be under the Jewish custom. Paul had no interest at all in causing any argument or disturbance over breaching a social custom. That was not the point. Since Timothy was a Jew, he would be treated as a Jew. But Titus was not a Jew, and so did not have to become one in order to know the gospel. He could receive the gospel straight out.

34

Paul had things to say about the "false brethren." There were those in the church whose ideas were wrong. To say they were "false brethren" does not necessarily mean they were insincere, or liars. They were "false" because what they were teaching was not true. There were those in the church at that time who were opposed to Paul and his way of preaching the gospel to the Gentiles. Paul called these men false because they had contradictory ideas which they brought in secretly, while they acted as if they were friends. They entered the group to see what Paul said and did, so that they could bring him under bondage. They were false in that they were not true believers in Christ.

Paul stood fast, refusing to make any concession to them. This example is important to Christian faith and life. The Christian has a personal relationship to God that is not dependent on any congregation or denomination. Paul refused to make any concession to anything that was not true to the gospel. He did this for the sake of his testimony. If Paul had given in, he would have denied the true gospel. "Silence pleads consent," and what men tolerate they are indirectly endorsing. If there are things being taught that are wrong, it is the duty of the Christian who knows the truth to point out the errors. The manner of doing this requires that the Lord should lead in the matter.

7

BEING PROMINENT DOES NOT MAKE A MAN RIGHT
(2:6-10)

Would you know that men may be prominent who cannot actually help you?

The truth in any message is not based on who says it, but on the effect it produces. Because of the human tendency to wish to be prominent, men tend to honor those who are prominent. Because a person is prominent does not mean that what he says is more true than what is said by some very humble person.

I grew up in a small rural community, and I can remember ideas that prevailed in that community. Some people were supposed to be better than others. There were certain families so prominent that if a person belonged to that family he was supposed to be something extra. If a person did not belong to that family, he just was not so good. I was one of those, by the way, that did not belong to any prominent family. As I was growing up I often asked myself, Why were certain families so special? Everyone seemed to say if those families were in favor of something, it was right; and if they were against it, it was wrong.

This can be true in a church. Many a congregation has its clique—the people who run it so to speak: little clusters of prominent people who pass the offices around among each other. This can be true with preachers, authors, and writers. But the question should be raised, What makes a person great? There need be no doubt that a person would be great if his preaching or writing helps in the winning of souls and the building up of faith.

In this regard, some men are counted great who do nothing of themselves: they discuss the things of the church but they never build one. They discuss evangelism yet never win souls. Such persons may be considered prominent in the church; yet they have never turned a single spadeful of real soil in the garden of God. Paul has this to say about some:

 But of these who seemed to be somewhat, (whatsoever they were, it maketh no matter to me: God accepteth no man's person:) for they who seemed to be somewhat in conference added nothing to me.—2:6

He met these so-called great men and did not get anything of significance from them.

But contrariwise, when they saw that the gospel of the

uncircumcision was committed unto me, as the gospel of the circumcision was unto Peter; (For he that wrought effectually in Peter to the apostleship of the circumcision, the same was mighty in me toward the Gentiles:) And when James, Cephas, and John, who seemed to be pillars, perceived the grace that was given unto me, they gave to me and Barnabas the right hands of fellowship; that we should go unto the heathen, and they unto the circumcision.— 2:7-9

There were of course really great men; but as far as Paul was concerned, he was not the least bit overawed by them.

It could be said Paul was mistaken: they really were great. But this did not matter, this was not Paul's business. He went by the Lord. When they saw Paul they shook hands with him and accepted him. They were not too proud to take him in. Paul notes this, "The gospel of the uncircumcision was committed unto me, as the gospel of circumcision was unto Peter." The "uncircumcision" refers to the Gentiles, and "circumcision" refers to the Jews.

When the gospel was preached in the Mediterranean world, and especially around Jerusalem, there were Jews as well as the rest of the people. The Jews would have no social dealings with anybody who wasn't a Jew. There was a sharp social division between Jews and Gentiles. The early church began to deal with the matter. It was decided that those who were in Christ were as one. In Christ there was neither Jew nor Greek, though out in the world there were Jews and there were Greeks. When the gospel is preached evangelistically, and so taken out into the world, it is the world we go by. Thus Peter was sent to the Jews, and Paul to the Gentiles. In Acts 15 the record shows that the early church did not go contrary to the social custom. This does not mean they necessarily endorsed it. Paul preached the gospel; Peter preached the gospel. God blessed them both.

Because God blessed them both, those great men, James, Peter and John, reached out their hands to this unknown person, Paul, and accepted him as a brother. Paul, who for fourteen years preached as an evangelist going over the country to far distant places, now came to Jerusalem and produced the evidence that God had actually blessed him. They reached out their hands, shook hands with him, and said, "You and we—we belong together."

PUBLIC CONDUCT
SHOULD BE CONSISTENT
(2:11-14)

Do you realize the importance of being consistent in the way you act?

Actions speak louder than words! "What you do speaks so loudly I cannot hear what you say." How often I have felt the truth of this. Witnessing for Christ and the gospel depends largely on the way a person acts before others. Part of the condemnation of the Pharisees by our Lord was this very fact: "They say, but they do not." James urges all, "Be ye doers of the word and not hearers only, deceiving your own selves."

In Galatians 2:11-14 is reported an occasion when Peter and others did not live up to their convictions, and Paul found it necessary to challenge them. The fact is that even among the apostles there could be differences of opinion. Paul and Barnabas had a famous disagreement and argument about whether or not Mark should go with them on the second missionary journey. Paul did not think Mark should go, but Barnabas differed, with the result that Barnabas went one way with Mark and Paul took Silas and went the other way.

"But when Peter was come to Antioch, I withstood him to the face, because he was to be blamed. For before that certain came

ate B/f communion

from James [who was in Jerusalem], he did eat with the Gentiles" (2:11, 12a). Apparently there were Gentiles in the church. The reason why Peter would eat with the Gentiles in the church was because they were no longer Gentiles and he was no longer a Jew. And so it would be that inside the Christian church, when they had their "love-feast" Peter did not hesitate to eat with the Gentiles. If Jews and Gentiles had eaten together in public it would have caused a big furor. Evidently inside the church this was acceptable.

When Christians came down from Jerusalem where James was the leader, "he [Peter] withdrew and separated himself, fearing them which were of the circumcision" (2:12b). He feared those in the church who had Jewish background.

> And the other Jews dissembled likewise with him; insomuch that Barnabas also was carried away with their dissimulation. But when I saw that they walked not uprightly according to the truth of the gospel, I said unto Peter before them all, If thou, being a Jew, livest after the manner of Gentiles, and not as do the Jews, why compellest thou the Gentiles to live as do the Jews?—2:13-14

Here we find that the issue was one of social appearance between the Jews and Gentiles. There is no indication that Peter did not know the truth—that the Gentiles were acceptable to God. The problem was that though he had known that, and had acted toward the Gentile Christians as if they were Christians and not Gentiles, then when these Jewish Christians from Jerusalem came to Antioch he changed his practice. He seems to have changed his practice because of social pressure. This may have been a human characteristic of Peter. The record shows that when he followed the Lord into Pilate's judgment hall a young girl accused him, "You're one of them that was with Jesus of Nazareth." And he replied, "No, I don't know the man." Later another said, "I know that you're one of them." Again he answered, "No, I don't know the man!" Then when a soldier said to him, "You are a Galilean, you talk like one. I know you're one of them," Peter began to swear that he did not know Jesus. This action in the church at Antioch could have been just a

Denial at arrest of Jesus

39

recurrence of his old human tendency—being so sensitive to what people thought of him that he actually faltered in living out his convictions.

Apparently Paul made an issue of this because Peter's conduct influenced others. When Peter withdrew, other Jewish Christians did too, even Barnabas. This great man, Barnabas, had known so well that the Gentiles were acceptable to God. Barnabas had been sent to Antioch, and he had seen how the Gentiles had become believers there. He had gone to find Saul, and he had brought Saul to teach these new believers. He had stayed there for two years and "the disciples were called Christians first at Antioch." When the Jewish Christians withdrew, Paul realized such action was hurting the testimony of the church. "But when I saw that they walked not uprightly according to the truth of the gospel"—that is to say, they did not live out what they really understood about the truth of the gospel, that in the Lord Jesus Christ there is neither Jew nor Gentile—"I said unto Peter before them all." Paul picked out the leading person because he was the one really responsible, and talked straight to him. Paul challenged this change of conduct because it gave the impression that Peter had changed his views. Peter had not really changed his views, but he had changed his conduct under social pressure. Paul's open challenge did not imply that Peter was wrong in his understanding; but Paul felt that Peter's conduct was inconsistent with the truth, and was giving a wrong impression to the public about the gospel of Christ.

Christians will always face this kind of social pressure. People will ask Christians about doctrinal matters, "Do you believe like this . . . do you believe like that?" They will often have their own names for it, saying, "Are you this kind of believer or are you that kind of believer?" At this point Christians should beware and make sure they act in line with the truth they know, so they may be consistent in their conduct and have a good testimony to all men before the Lord.

PART FOUR

HOW MAN
IS JUSTIFIED

(2:15–3:14)

9

"NOT BY WORKS BUT BY FAITH"
(2:15-19)

Do you know what it means to be "justified by faith"?

"Justified by the faith of Christ" is the great truth in the gospel. In the Book of Galatians Paul gives a description of the gospel: "Our Lord Jesus Christ, Who gave himself for our sins, that he might deliver us from this present evil world, according to the will of God and our Father" (1:3b, 4). There is an underlying truth in the very nature of things that makes this gospel necessary. God is holy. This is an eternal, essential, everlasting fact. "He is of purer eyes than to behold evil," and "He will by no means clear the guilty." It is this which causes trouble at once. God is holy, and men are sinners. Sin alienates the soul from God. Sin disqualifies the soul from fellowship with God. Something needs to be done. The soul needs to be *just* in the eyes of God. The word *just* means being all a person should be. The words *just* and *righteousness* have practically the same meaning. The soul that desires to draw nigh unto God must be made just. This is true for everyone, since "all have sinned and come short of the glory of God." But from the time of Abraham, it has been known that the way of salvation is by faith. "Abraham believed God, and it was counted to him for righteousness."

It seems that some take this Scripture to mean that if a person has faith there will be no need of righteousness. But this is a perversion of the truth of the gospel. Believing in Christ is the source of righteousness, because of what Jesus Christ has already done. He came into this world, took on a human form, suffered and died on the cross of Calvary, was raised from the dead, ascended into the presence of God, where He now is interceding for those who believe in Him. When a soul believes in Jesus Christ, the benefits of Christ's work on earth, on the cross, in the resurrection, at the right hand of God, sending the Holy Spirit, His coming again, His present intercession—in fact, all the benefits of Jesus Christ are already available to the Christian. Believing in Christ Jesus, accepting Him as Savior, confessing Him as Lord, means accepting Calvary and the resurrection and Pentecost and the coming again of Jesus Christ as true. And accepting these historic facts involves obeying the will of the Lord Jesus Christ now.

When a person receives the Holy Spirit into his heart, the Holy Spirit will take the things of Christ and show them to the believer. Believing in Christ Jesus opens the heart to receive the Holy Spirit, who activates the will of Jesus Christ in the life of the believer. It is this truth that enabled Paul to write, "For as many as are led by the Spirit of God, they are the sons of God" (Rom. 8:14). This is the real, actual truth; and this is the meaning of "being justified," made just. A person is not "made just" simply by wiping out his guilt. A person is not righteous and just until he is doing what is right: this is possible only in Christ Jesus.

Paul reminds the Galatians:

> We who are Jews by nature, and not sinners of the Gentiles,
> Knowing that a man is not justified by the works of the
> law, but by the faith of Jesus Christ, even we have believed
> in Jesus Christ, that we might be justified by the faith of
> Christ, and not by the works of the law: for by the works
> of the law shall no flesh be justified.—2:15-16

A sinner does not become righteous in the presence of God by his efforts to keep what the law prescribes. The law of God is the outward expression of what the nature of God demands. Since God is holy, He requires certain things from man. These requirements have been expressed in the Ten Words on Mount Sinai, commonly called the law of God. A man may take them as goals before him and try to keep them. Such trying to keep them is "works," and no one will ever succeed. It is because of this inability that a man is not justified by his own efforts. He can never become righteous, he can never be just. "Being just" means not only that his sins are forgiven; it means that he has operating in him the active will of God. The believer is actually doing God's will; and no man can accomplish this by his own effort, but only by faith in Jesus Christ. Through believing in Jesus Christ a person can have "Christ in you, the hope of glory." When he believes in Jesus Christ he becomes attached to Him, so that Christ is the Head and the believer is the body. Christ is the Vine and believers are the branches. *Jn 15*

It is by believing in Christ that, by the grace of God working in the believer through the Holy Spirit, the Christian will be moved into the will of God. Of course, when a person receives Christ Jesus he receives the forgiveness of sin. God ascribes to him the righteousness of Jesus Christ because the believer now belongs to Him. As the bride who marries a king inherits his kingdom, so believers are members of the Bride of Christ and share in the righteousness of Christ.

To whom does God impute this righteousness? He imputes this righteousness to those who in His sight are justified: those who are yielded to Christ, in whom the Holy Spirit is working to produce the things of Christ. Because of this, it is right in the sight of God for a sinner to repent, to forsake his sins, and to cast himself on the mercy of God. In doing this the sinner enters into a working operation with God: God "works in me to will and to do of his good pleasure." This is how a person is viewed in the sight of God; in this way a sinner is justified.

The "works of the law" are those actions undertaken when a person considers what God requires. No one can do those works of himself. No one is good enough, wise enough, nor strong enough. It is just not in the natural man to do the things of God. But "Christ in you" can do this. When the Lord Jesus Christ comes to the sinner, he is born again, he now has the life of God in him, and thus is enabled by the grace of God to walk in His ways. Being justified, made just, God will ascribe to the believer the righteousness of Jesus

Christ, which he now can have by faith. Actions which the believer now undertakes in obedience to His will are undergirded by the One who loved him and gave Himself for him.

10

CHRIST
LIVETH IN ME
(2:19-20)

Do you understand how a Christian can consider himself a failure that he might be a success?

The living of a Christian in this world is never the result of human effort. If there is a real Christian in the family, all will know what a low opinion such a person usually has of himself. When anyone would try to tell such a person how good he is and how fine he is, that Christian would be embarrassed because the Christian knows his conduct is not his own doing. Other people may admire Christians and praise them, but all the time the Christians are so humble. This is not false pretense. That is the way they really feel. Because right here is the central truth in all Christians' spiritual experience. Their conduct is not of themselves; it is from the Lord.

Paul continues to discuss this truth in words that are familiar and profound: "For I through the law am dead to the law, that I might live unto God" (2:19). The word "law" as it is used by the apostle Paul means the expressed will of God. The law of God was written as Scripture: the Ten Words on Mount Sinai. The law of God is God's way of doing things. Paul writes, "I through the law [i.e., according to the will of God] am dead to the law." In what sense would he be dead through the law? According to the law, the Ten Commandments, he is a sinner. And as a sinner, he would in himself be destroyed; but here Paul writes like a Christian. For the Christian there is more to the law of God than judgment on sin. Scripture not only teaches the will of God with reference to conduct, but it also shows the will of God with reference to confession of sin and the forgiveness of sin. There is revealed the whole worship procedure wherein the believer comes before God as a sinner and brings a sacrifice: a life to be taken in place of his own. Death of the sacrifice will be involved, so that the sinner is reckoned as if he had died. The blood of the sacrifice is accepted as though the sinner had died according to the penalty of his sin. Now he is reckoned as if he was dead.

The Word of God and the will of God for the believer in the New Testament is that he should deny himself: "If any man will be my disciple, let him deny himself, take up his cross and follow me" (Matt. 16:24). So through the express will of God, the believer is dead to the law in this sense, that he counts himself to be dead: his human nature is counted to be dead. And if his human nature is dead, then temptations can no longer reach him. The believer is not susceptible to temptation because his human nature is dead. So Paul could write, "I am dead to the law that I might live unto God."

This truth is even more clearly stated in verse 20, where Paul writes, "I am crucified with Christ." He means that by faith he belongs to the Lord Jesus Christ, and he accepts in the Lord Jesus Christ death to himself even as it came to Him. The believer joins Him on Calvary's cross and reckons himself indeed to be dead. He reckons himself to be dead by faith; it is an exercise of faith. "I am crucified with Christ" in the flesh; "nevertheless I live." He was Paul the apostle. He was a missionary. He was a teacher and a preacher. But he says, "Yet not I, but Christ liveth in me." "Yet not I," in the sense of his human ego. He was not the old Saul the Pharisee, "but Christ liveth in me." There is a new life in him, and it is the life of Christ.

When the believer says, "Christ liveth in me," he means that Christ is now making the choices, the selections; He is making the decisions. So Paul continues, "The life which I now live in the flesh": denying himself, yielding to the will of God, responding to the Holy Spirit, obeying God, serving God—all these things are done in the flesh. Paul took his flesh in hand: he buffeted his body and kept it in subjection (I Cor. 9:27). He made his flesh "a hewer of wood and a drawer of water." He made his flesh obey, even as Christ Jesus made His flesh obey. Christ Jesus took His flesh to Calvary's cross, and the sinner takes his flesh in self-crucifixion with God. "The life which I now live in the flesh [a continuous self-denial] I live by the faith of the Son of God." The way Paul was able to do this was by believing in the Lord Jesus Christ, because then Christ was in him. Paul responded to Him by receiving Him into himself; and the Holy Spirit was given to make Christ real in him. This is the truth Paul had in mind when he prayed for the Ephesians "to be strengthened with might by his Spirit in the inner man; that Christ may dwell in your hearts by faith" (Eph. 3:16-17). This is why he writes to the Colossians, "Christ in you, the hope of glory" (Col. 1:27).

Think of a pianist sitting down at a piano to play. Anyone hitting a key can make a sound. Some can hit the keys and produce only noise. But some can sit down to that piano and by touching the right chord, playing the right notes together in certain combinations, can make sweet sounds. Suppose a person sits down to a piano with his hands over the keys. Now picture a master pianist inside that person. The master can put his hands on the hands of that person, his fingers on those fingers so that by some means he can guide the fingers to the right keys at the right time, so that it would appear that the person sitting on the stool was playing the piano. This is how a Christian lives. Christ Jesus is in him, moving the Christian as to what to do and how to do it, when to say it and how to say it. A Christian person in the home acts the way he is inwardly led; the Christian woman in the community acts the way she is inwardly led; a Christian young person in school acts the way he or she is led. This is because the Christian is led from within by the Holy Spirit of God, who makes the things of Christ real to him. "Christ liveth in me." "Christ in you, the hope of glory."

11

CHRISTIAN LIVING IS BY THE HOLY SPIRIT
(2:21–3:3)

Do you realize that (if) anybody could do right in his human nature, then Christ's death on Calvary was unnecessary?

Salvation is the work of God. It is not by the effort of man. It takes place in man and it affects man's conduct and activities, but it doesn't start from man. This is the very essence of the gospel of Jesus Christ. To understand the gospel, one must realize that man in himself cannot do the will of God. Man is a sinner condemned as unrighteous and is counted as unfit.

All this was known to God, and this is the background from which God sent Jesus Christ to save man. The Son of God came as Jesus of Nazareth; and being God Himself in human form, He was inwardly obedient in every way, obeying perfectly the will of His Father.

In the Book of Hebrews it is written that He learned obedience through suffering: "Though he were a Son, yet learned he obedience by the things which he suffered" (Heb. 5:8). In order to die in the flesh, He actually took His body to the cross and there died. The resurrection actually happened to His human, physical body; and He later ascended to be in fellowship with His Father, as He is now. All this was done in vicarious fashion. The word *vicarious* means that one person does something for another person. All of the Lord Jesus' perfect living was done for me. By faith, a sinner can receive this, so that I could be one with Christ. This is called the atonement. The word *atonement* means at-one-ment. Strictly it means to be at one with the Lord. The atonement brings the sinner and Christ together as one. Now this communion, this being at one with Christ, is in a very true way entering into partnership with Him. In another way you could say "grafted in as a wild olive tree branch is grafted into a tame olive tree." It is this matter of becoming a member of the family, of joining Him, of being married to Him, of being members of His Bride that is confirmed by the Holy Spirit. The Holy Spirit is given to believers to blend the human being and Christ together in one. The Holy Spirit takes the will of the Lord Jesus Christ and makes it active in the heart of the believer.

To speak about joining the Lord Jesus Christ, so that He and I become one, does not mean He is going to change His ways. He does not join the believer on a give and take basis. He does not take a little of Himself and a little of me and thereby make a new person. No, that is not the way it is. He takes me over into Himself. He is the Vine, I am the branch. The life that is from Him is a total, complete life. I yield myself to Him as empty and needy. I come to Him totally ready to receive Him, and it is He that lives in me. This communion is confirmed by the Holy Spirit. The Holy Spirit activates in me the will of the living Lord.

All this begins in an experience ordinarily called "conversion." It is the beginning of the spiritual life in Christ. The believer is now a "babe in Christ." This is the beginning of things! But newborn babes are expected to grow. Peter says, "As newborn babes, desire the sincere milk of the word, that ye may grow thereby" (I Peter 2:2). Babies grow, to become full-grown, mature persons in their consecration.

In Galatia, the people had heard the gospel from Paul. They had believed in the Lord Jesus Christ, and they had this new life in them by the grace of God. Just as surely as anyone receives Him, he will have eternal life. The promise is so simple that a child can understand it. And it is true, that far more takes place than can ever be understood. A man must be born again. A new thing will begin in the believer, and that new thing is the life of Christ. The Holy Spirit will be given to the believer and the believer will grow. Spiritual things will become stronger. Human nature will be more under control, as the believer dies to self. Feeding the spirit and putting the flesh to death, the Christian will grow spiritually according to the plan of God.

In Galatia, however, the other preachers were saying, "You began your Christian life by believing in the Lord Jesus Christ, and that was good. Then you received the Holy Spirit of God and you were blessed in Him, and that was good. But now there are things you must do." They outlined regulations. If the believer would keep all these regulations he would be good; then he would be doing what God wanted him to do. This is what bothered Paul because it is not true. Paul argued with them. "I do not frustrate the grace of God [what I am teaching is not contrary to what God wants to do for you] : for if righteousness come by the law, then Christ is dead in vain" (2:21). And of course, that is not true! "O foolish Galatians, who hath bewitched you, that ye should not obey the truth, before whose eyes Jesus Christ hath been evidently set forth, crucified among you?" (3:1). They had had clear preaching of the gospel. They had had a vivid preaching of the fact that Jesus Christ had died for them. Paul went on to write: "This only would I learn of you, Received ye the Spirit by the works of the law, or by the hearing of faith?" (3:2).

In other words, these people had received the Holy Spirit, not by working for Him, but because they had believed the promises of God. So Paul asks, "Are ye so foolish? having begun in the Spirit, are ye now made perfect by the flesh?" (3:3). This is the way he tries to keep them from making a mistake. After all, they had received the Holy Spirit by believing. They had become Christians by believing in Christ. Why in the world should they now think they should work for their salvation? A human being can't do it in himself; it is "Christ in you, the hope of glory." Paul is going to press this point. Now everything in Christ Jesus is for you. You turn to Him, come to Him, and He will give it to you. His righteousness is yours; you are to trust Him. You cannot earn it! He will give it to you as a gift. The "free gift of God is eternal life through Jesus Christ our Lord."

12

THE GALATIANS
HAD STARTED RIGHT
(3:4-5)

Do you think Christian living is by the Christian's own strength?

Christian living is something far different than the world would think. I can understand this, as I was a grown man when I became a believer. I used to have the idea that a Christian was a person who was trying to be good—like a person would cut out weeds from a garden. By cutting out all evil, such a person would become better and better. Thus a person would become a Christian as he would discipline the flesh, and make himself clean, neat, sweet, and good. The idea was that being a Christian was an achievement, the result of a resolution on my part. I was encouraged to hold such a view because many people would make it obvious they were doing their best, and would say, "I don't see why things don't turn out well with me, because I'm doing everything I possibly can." All this is "works" and such efforts would be in my own strength. But this is not the gospel. In speaking of works the Bible says, "All our righteousnesses are as filthy rags."

The Christian begins by denying himself. "If any man will come after me, let him deny himself, take up his cross, and follow me" (Matt. 16:24). A person must acknowledge that he cannot control himself, nor train himself so that he will be just a little better than he is now. He must reckon himself dead in the sight of God, and deny himself, that he might belong to the Lord Jesus Christ. Paul tells the Galatians of his own spiritual experience: "I am crucified with Christ: nevertheless I live; yet not I, but Christ liveth in me: and the life which I now live in the flesh I live by the faith of the Son of God, who loved me, and gave himself for me" (2:20).

So the Christian starts by saying, "I am crucified with Christ."

52

This involves yielding to the will of God, accepting what comes, and praising God. This means accepting suffering when that comes and trusting God. "Have ye suffered so many things in vain? if it be yet in vain." When the Galatians became Christians they suffered. It is important that every Christian understand that if he is going to walk with the Lord and seek His face, "All that will live godly in Christ Jesus shall suffer persecution."

The persecution will come in various forms. Perhaps a believer wants to live the life of faith in the Lord Jesus Christ by having prayer in the home. Everyone may not be in favor of that. Suppose the believer wants to have Bible reading in the family fellowship; do all agree? One should not be surprised to find resistance. When a person tries to live the Christian life, there will be those who take advantage of you. That is part of the suffering that comes to the believer who wants to promote spiritual things.

There is a very interesting description of the Galatians' pastor: "He therefore that ministereth to you the Spirit, and worketh miracles among you, doeth he it by the works of the law, or by the hearing of faith?" (3:5). That pastor ministered the Holy Spirit to them. His preaching resulted in men getting to know about the Holy Spirit. His preaching and his praying resulted in their yielding themselves to the Holy Spirit. He ministered the Spirit to them and he worked miracles among them. He prayed for them, and he exercised his faith on their behalf to get results.

Paul comments on the work of their pastor: "Doeth he it by the works of the law?" This man who accomplished these things among them spiritually, was he doing this by teaching the law? Was this man getting up and telling them, "You'd better be good. You'd better do right"? If he had done that he would have been preaching the law, and Paul emphasized that that is not the way a person will receive the Holy Spirit. The person receives the Holy Spirit of God because the person believes in Him. Because he believes in the Lord Jesus Christ, he will receive the Holy Spirit, whom the Lord Jesus Christ will send to believers. Looking into the face of Jesus Christ will show the soul how much he needs to know Him. "The Holy Spirit will take the things of the Lord Jesus Christ and show them unto you." When the Spirit comes into a person there will be a light in the soul, there will be strength in the walk, and there will be inward encouragement and help as the believer goes his way.

When Paul raises the question, "Doeth he it [that is, the ministering of the Spirit] by the works of the law, or by the hearing of faith?" he is asking the Galatians to reflect on the witness of their pastor. "Is he telling you to do good deeds, or is he telling you to believe what God has done?" There may seem to be scarcely any difference here. Such an impression will reveal that a person has not tried it. If a person will look into what Paul has written, he will see that there is a big difference between a person working for something he can never earn, and receiving it as a gift. All the things that are true about the Lord Jesus Christ and the Holy Spirit will be brought to mind when a person looks into the face of his Savior. And the Holy Spirit will be very close when the believer starts looking into the face of his Lord. When a believer looks into the face of Jesus Christ and begins to realize He is alive, and that the believer can have fellowship with Him, God will move in the heart to do His will and will draw the believer closer and closer to Him. Instead of having the works of the law which emphasize reward and punishment, such a person will have promise and blessing. God will do it for any person who will put his trust in the Lord Jesus Christ.

13

BELIEVING WAS
ABRAHAM'S WAY
(3:6-9)

Do you realize that receiving from God as a gift all that you need and want has always been the truth of the gospel?

Salvation is the work of God. We say this over and over again; we can never say it too often. Everything that happens in salvation is something that God does. He does it freely, gladly, but *He* does it.

Salvation, as the work of God, was first experienced by Abraham; and he has been called "the father of the faithful." This means to say that he was the first one who walked by faith, and all others who have walked by faith since his time are accounted his children. He was the pioneer in living in faith, so far as the Bible is concerned. The truth of this principle of living by faith can be seen in Abraham's career. Perhaps this can best be seen by contrasting the way Abraham lived with the way the men of Babel went about building the tower. The story of the Tower of Babel is recorded in Genesis 11, and in chapter 12 the story of Abraham begins. In Genesis 11 it is recorded that men got together and encouraged each other to make brick and build a tower and a city. They wanted to build a city lest they be scattered; they wanted to build a tower that would reach to heaven. In this way they undertook to make something worthwhile by their own efforts. In chapter 12 is written the story of Abraham who wanted the same things the men of Babel wanted. He, like the men of Babel, sought security. The difference between Abraham and the men of Babel can be seen in what the men of Babel said to each other:

> And they said one to another, Go to, let us make brick, and burn them thoroughly. And they had brick for stone, and slime had they for mortar. And they said, Go to, let us build us a city and a tower, whose top may reach unto heaven; and let us make us a name, lest we be scattered abroad upon the face of the whole earth.—Gen. 11:3-4

But it is recorded of Abraham: "For he looked for a city which hath foundations, whose builder and maker is God" (Heb. 11:10). Right here is the very heart of the gospel of Jesus Christ. This is the real truth, the central idea in the mind of a Christian. The believer is looking to Jesus Christ for the very things that he needs and values in life.

One philosophy of life is for a person to do his best to get and make all he can, so that he will have something tangible to hold on to. The other way of living is to look up to God and to receive from Him everything He wants to give you. The Christian will say that if a person will look up to God and receive from Him everything God is willing to give, he will have more than he needs. In this world a person may never have things the way he would like to have them. As a matter of fact, "In the world ye shall have tribulation" (John 16:33); and men live in situations in this world where things are generally imperfect. Men are not big enough, strong enough, smart enough, and will not live long enough to get everything gathered together the way in which they want it. The Christian is comforted by the words of the Lord Jesus: "Be of good cheer, I have overcome the world" (John 16:33).

There are two ways to go about facing the problems of living in this world. One way is to try to do it in one's own strength and wisdom. A person can try to do the very best he can; be as smart as he can; be as strong as he knows how. He can collect and save; do and have; keep and build. That is one way. Another way is to look up to God. Trust in Him. This does not mean the believer will not work. It does not mean he will not go and do. But it does mean he will not worry about things. He will not depend on himself. He will look to God to do for him. The second way is the Christian way. It is based on the conviction that God has prepared and is willing to provide everything the believer needs or wants.

What needs to be done now, so far as the Christian is concerned, is for him to see what God has done. This whole line of truth comes out in Galatians 3:6-9 as it is shown in the life of Abraham. "Even as Abraham believed God, and it was accounted to him for righteousness" (3:6). When it is written that he believed God, it means much more than to say he believed there was a God. Certainly he did that; and he not only believed that God was real, but also that He was powerful and He was strong. Also he believed that God was great and holy and merciful. All that could be true, but this statement means more than that. "Abraham believed God" the way in which a servant believes a master, when the servant *does* what the master says. Abraham took God's word as real; and when God told him to come out, he came out. When God told him to go, he went. The record is that "by faith Abraham obeyed and went out, not knowing whither he went."

This obedience was included in believing God. "Abraham believed God," trusted in God, "and it was accounted to him for righteousness." This word "accounted" means more than just a matter of bookkeeping. He believed in God; and believing in God became the source of his conduct, which was righteous before God. "Know ye therefore that they which are of faith, the same are the children of Abraham" (3:7). To say "they which are of faith" means that their way of living is by faith. These are persons who live their lives believing in the promises of God. "The same are the children of Abraham" in the sense that they live as he lived; they resemble him. Children resemble their parents. As they grow up in their homes, they act like their parents. And so those who are of faith live like Abraham, act like Abraham. "And the scripture, foreseeing that God would justify the heathen through faith, preached before the gospel unto Abraham, saying, In thee shall all nations be blessed" (3:8). It was always in the will of God that He would bring anyone into the state of being righteous before Him when that person believed in Him. God would do this in response to faith in His promises.

The whole experience of a Christian starts with the fact that God gives a promise, the believer responds to the promise, and as he believes in Him, God works in him "to will and do of his good pleasure." "In thee shall all nations be blessed" means that in Abraham's way of living, all nations—everybody on the face of the earth—would be blessed. This is the eternal plan for all mankind. There are not two or three different ways of getting right with God. The way to get right with God is to trust in Him and believe in Him.

"So then they which be of faith are blessed with faithful Abraham" (3:9). It follows then that anyone who lives according to the promises of God in Christ Jesus today will be blessed of God, even as Abraham was blessed in that he was a believing, obedient man. That is the way it will be for any person who believes. "God is, and that God is a rewarder of them that diligently seek Him." The Christian is thinking about God, he is trusting in God. So far as his family is concerned, he thinks about God. So far as his neighbors are concerned, he thinks about God. So far as his business is concerned, he thinks about God. So far as his school work is concerned, he thinks about God. God is in everything. God is everywhere. The Christian has trust in Him. The Christian is depending on Him, and God's attitude toward him is one of mercy and grace. He gave His Son to die for the sins of the Christian. He gave His Son to rise from the dead for the Christian. Christ Jesus is the Savior, and He will bless the soul who trusts in Him.

14

THIS IS WHAT
SCRIPTURE TEACHES
(3:10-11)

Did you know that the Bible never teaches you to work for blessing?

Salvation is the free gift of God. But the Christian is going to have to work to eat. He will work for his daily food. The Christian will plow the fields and will scatter the seed in order to raise a crop. "And whatsoever a man soweth, that shall he also reap" is the law that prevails so far as day-in-and-day-out living is concerned.

Receiving blessings from God is a good deal like belonging to a family. A child does not work to be a son. A little girl does not work to be a daughter. They belong to the parents. So it is with reference to the things of God. If a person belongs to God, he belongs to Him! And it will be the free gift of God that brings salvation: God will save to the uttermost those that come to Him through the Lord Jesus Christ (Heb. 7:25).

It has been noted above that there are just two ways of securing anything in a legitimate way. One of these ways is to work for it. And there are many things in the world for which a person will have to work. But there is another way of securing things, and that is to receive them as gifts. It is natural to feel that a person should earn what he expects to acquire. In a way it is flattering to feel that one should earn what one gets, because then when he works he would have some praise for it. Yet it follows that on this basis, the person is going to get just what he works for. It will follow that he will reap what he sows.

This can be a very sobering fact when it comes to spiritual things, because if a person should make a mistake, he would get the penalty. If a person was living on the basis of "whatsoever a man soweth that shall he also reap" and he lived through a day not thinking about God, it would result in that person not having God. It becomes obvious the soul will need something far more than that. Human beings need the ever faithful God who stands by them even when they are not faithful to Him. Because on the basis of the law of getting what a person deserves, nothing but total achievement could possibly be adequate. Since "all have sinned and come short of the glory of God," this way is hopeless so far as man is concerned.

Scripture has always set forth a different principle than the law when it comes to spiritual things.

> For as many as are of the works of the law are under the curse: for it is written, Cursed is every one that continueth not in all things which are written in the book of the law to do them. But that no man is justified by the law in the sight of God, it is evident: for, The just shall live by faith.— 3:10-11

The word "just" refers to the people who are righteous in God's sight. "The just shall live by faith" means by faith in God through Christ Jesus. When a person believes in the Lord Jesus Christ and His promises, the result will be that that person will be right in God's sight. Believing followed as a way of life will ensure receiving what is promised from God. The word "faith" is the noun of which the word "believing" is the verb, and either "faith" or "believing" designates the action that brings a person into blessing. "The just shall live by faith" has always been true. If a person wanted to be "right" in the sight of God, the "rightness" in him, the "rightness" in his conduct, his heart, soul, and mind would be the result of the fact that he believed in God. He would receive his "rightness" from God.

Believing is to the soul what swallowing is to the body. Now swallowing is something a person does. When it is said that swallowing is the way one lives, what is really meant is swallowing food, not just any substance. A person could swallow poison, but that would be fatal. The same thing is true of believing. When it is said "the just shall live by faith," it is meant that the just man will live by believing the promises of God. It does not mean believing anything and everything. As a person can swallow poison to his hurt; so he can believe error to his hurt. Both will be fatal. Believing in the Lord Jesus Christ brings life eternal, and that is vital.

To say, "It doesn't make any difference what you believe, just so you believe," means that one might just as well say, "It doesn't make any difference what you swallow." But that is obviously false. It's *what* a person believes that makes the difference. Or should it be said *whom* a person believes makes the difference? Believing only commits the person to the things in which he believes. If he happens to believe the right thing, he is fortunate. If he believes the wrong thing, he's fooled. How is anybody ever cheated? How does one person ever take advantage of another? Is it not true that one person believes in the other? It happens when one believes another person is honest, when he actually is not. Believing in his honesty did not make him honest. It does make a difference whom one believes, what one believes; even so with reference to the things of God. It makes a difference whether a person believes in Him.

"Now the just man shall live by faith." That is true. But it is faith in the Lord Jesus Christ. "For as many as are of the works of the law" refers to people who are depending on doing things to get right with God. They are going to fail. "For it is written, Cursed is every one that continueth not in all things which are written in the book of the law to do them." This means that if a person is missing in one point, he is guilty of it all. "But that no man is justified by the law."

It never was intended that way; no one ever gets right by doing the things that the law requires, but by faith. "But that no man is justified by the law in the sight of God, it is evident: for, The just shall live by faith." This was Martin Luther's great text. He found out that a person could be righteous and just by believing in the Lord Jesus Christ, and that is still true. When a person puts his faith in the Lord Jesus Christ and trusts in Him, God will make him what he ought to be. God will bless him.

15

THE BLESSING
OF ABRAHAM
(3:12-14)

Do you realize that the benefits of the Christian gospel are available only through Jesus Christ personally?

Salvation is by faith. By salvation is meant all that God will do for any soul who will receive Jesus Christ. What God will do in Christ involves the daily living of the believer, how he acts and reacts as he goes along day by day. Will he do this because he prefers it, or because God wills it? This is the question and it will include his family, business, school, community. In other words, a person will act either according to what seems good to him or according to the way in which he feels inwardly led by God. Salvation is operative in this second way. Certain consequences will always follow, with various kinds of experiences for the person in anything he does. Some of these consequences would be counted as blessings, when the believer has joy and gladness of heart. Such blessings come to those who believe in God. "And the law is not of faith: but, The man that doeth them shall live in them" (3:12).

The word *law* is used with several meanings in the Bible. Usually it is used to indicate the Ten Commandments, the law of Moses. Or it may be used to refer to the Bible as a whole, "the law." Sometimes the reference is to the revelation of God in His Word, which can be designated as "the law." Then again a person may have in mind God's way of doing things, in which "whatsoever a man soweth, that shall he also reap," so that things come out according to their nature. That can also be called "the law."

In all these uses, however, the comment made by Paul is true: "Now the law is not of faith." It is clear "that whatsoever a man soweth, that shall he also reap." When a person is attempting to do things in his own strength, he is not exercising faith. In saying "the law is not of faith," the word "faith" does not mean "make believe." Faith is never a case of doing nothing as over against striving. Faith is related to the Lord Jesus Christ. It is a matter of entering into personal relationship with the Lord Jesus in such a way that Christ will live His life in you. The believer will appear to be active, but it will be Christ who is actually active in him. The believer will work and struggle and labor, but the guidance of his thinking will not be his own; it will be from the Lord Jesus Christ. If a person is living according to faith, according to what he believes, it will be a matter of being yielded to the Person of the Lord Jesus Christ so that He is carrying out His will in the believer. But Paul points out: "And the law is not of faith: but, The man that doeth them shall live in them." When the person is acting according to his own judgment, the consequences will be related directly to what he does.

"Christ hath redeemed us from the curse of the law, being made a curse for us: for it is written, Cursed is every one that hangeth on a tree" (3:13). The significant fact is that "Christ hath redeemed us from the curse of the law." One must be very careful who is included in the "us." "Christ hath redeemed us": not all mankind, but those who believe. He has redeemed Christians—"us"—"from the curse of the law." The curse of the law is clear: "The soul that sinneth, it shall die." When it is said, "Christ hath redeemed us," the idea is that Christ came in as "the Lamb of God," and "bore in his own body" the judgment of the believer's conduct. By His dying for sinners He, as it were, paid the penalty for error, for sins; and He bore away the judgment on believers. The law would say, "The soul that sinneth, it shall die"; but Christ Jesus came in and died. Since death is what the curse of the law was, He bore it away; and thus His death becomes operative for believers. It is an amazing way that God works in accepting the death of Jesus Christ in place of the death of the guilty party.

"That the blessing of Abraham might come on the Gentiles through Jesus Christ; that we might receive the promise of the Spirit through faith" (3:14). In other words, Christ has redeemed us from the curse of the law, so that the blessing of Abraham might come on the Gentiles through faith. The death of the Lord Jesus Christ makes it possible for a sinner, with a weight of guilt against him, to be forgiven. Any believing man will be forgiven for Christ's sake, and then he can also by faith commit himself to the living Lord Jesus Christ. Christ Jesus will actually live in him, live His life in him, in such a way that the blessing of Abraham will be actually operative in that particular man. What then is the blessing of Abraham that is written about in verse 14? Apparently the promise of the Spirit is the blessing of Abraham.

But what is the promise of the Spirit? That God will live in the believer, to work in him, to guide him, and to bless him. Some of the promises in the covenant with Abraham in the Old Testament are "I will be with thee, whithersoever thou goest, I will keep thee and I will bring thee to this land that I will give thee." And all those actions of God take place in the believer's life: "I will be with thee, I will keep thee, I will bring thee, I will give thee." God will be performing what He had promised to Abraham. He also says, "Whosoever blesses thee, I will bless, and whosoever curses thee I will curse." By this He is saying, "I will protect thee."

God will come and dwell with His people. He will watch over them and keep them and protect them and strengthen them. And this is the meaning of Scripture when it says, " . . . that we might receive the promise of the Spirit through faith." The promise of the Spirit is God working in the believer "to will and to do of his good pleasure," with Christ Jesus showing the things of God and strengthening the believer in faith so that he may obey Him. Apparently this was the promise of the Spirit, and this is made available by the Lord Jesus Christ because He died and set man free from sin. He set men free from sin by this very device: dying for them and then being raised from the dead, making it possible that by believing in Him a person can be crucified with Christ, can be raised from the dead, and can share with Him in all the benefits He has available. "The blessing of Abraham" means God will be with the believer and Christ Jesus will be with the believer and the Holy Spirit will be in the heart of each believer, "whosoever will."

PART FIVE

GOD'S PROMISES
vs.
GOD'S LAWS

(3:15—4:2)

16

THE ORIGINAL
PURPOSE OF GOD
(3:15-17)

Do you realize that it was always the purpose of God to give freely whatever man needed for blessing?

Salvation is the work of God for and in a man by which the man can live in His will and be blessed. Through salvation, the believer is enabled to walk in the ways of God and to have fellowship with God by the indwelling of the Holy Spirit of God, who brings the life of the Lord Jesus Christ into the heart of the individual.

Somehow it seems natural to think that this plan of salvation was provided after man had failed in his own efforts. It is as though the original plan of God would have been for man to achieve his own benefits; but as man failed to do this because of sin, God provided salvation as a sort of substitute for those who were lost. Yet that is not the way it happened. In the Bible it is revealed that Christ Jesus was "the Lamb slain from the foundation of the world" (Rev. 13:8). This shows that God had in mind from the very beginning—before He ever made this world—that persons living in His presence should do so by His grace and mercy. It is quite natural to feel that if a man is well and strong and able to earn his living, it would be proper to say, "He is doing very well." What is not always realized is that he could not do a thing if it were not given to him of God. God supplies the strength that the man uses in daily living. God supplies the ability to learn and to do. All that a person is or has or can hope to be is from God.

This does not mean that a man is to do the will of God to the best of his ability; and then when he fails, Christ Jesus will come along to help him. The original plan and purpose of God was that man should serve God by the grace of God, that God would give him what he needs spiritually in just the same way that God gives him what he needs physically. It is common to think that the law of Moses, the Ten Commandments, which shows men how to live, was given after men had done wrong, after they had lost their way and had become confused, to straighten them out, as a sort of restorative procedure. This idea is not true. The law of Moses is eternal. It was always true, grounded in the very nature of God. It would be a mistake for any man to think that by keeping the law he could earn the blessing of God. That never was the intention in revealing the Ten Words. Actually, it is the free gift of the blessing of God in the person of the Holy Spirit that enables anyone to keep the law.

In Galatians 3:15-17 Paul emphasizes that living in the Lord Jesus Christ, depending on the grace of God to live successfully in His presence, is an old, old idea. God had that in mind when He first created this world. "Brethren, I speak after the manner of men; Though it be but a man's covenant, yet if it be confirmed, no man disannulleth, or addeth thereto" (3:15). This means to say that if any arrangement "be but a man's covenant," a human contract, "if it be confirmed," if men have started working on it, "no man disannulleth, or addeth thereto." Men do not change it. Nobody alters it at will.

> Now to Abraham and his seed were the promises made. He saith not, And to seeds, as of many; but as of one, And to thy seed, which is Christ. And this I say, that the covenant, that was confirmed before of God in Christ, the law, which was four hundred and thirty years after, cannot disannul, that it should make the promise of none effect.—3:16-17

The original purpose of God was to bless all men through the seed of Abraham (Gen. 12:3), which is through Christ Jesus. And the law, which was given to Moses 430 years afterward, would not change this original principle. The general principle Paul is expounding is that when an agreement has been reached and confirmed, nobody can alter it at will, adding to or taking from it. In the discussion of God's promise to Abraham, Paul holds that this promise has been confirmed in Christ. Thus the principle of receiving the blessing of God by grace from God was included in God's eternal plan for man. Paul made much of the fact that the word "seed" is in the singular. This indicated that the saving grace of God is not a general principle but a specific agreement. "He saith not, And to seeds, as of many; but as of one, And to thy seed, which is Christ" (3:16). The promise that God made to Abraham did not go out to all men directly, but only through Christ.

The promise made to Abraham, that God would bless him and his seed, did not refer to all mankind but only to Abraham and his seed. It referred to the Lord Jesus Christ specifically, as the Seed of Abraham. Since God made that promise to Abraham and had begun to operate along that line, the law of Moses could not change it. God had worked that way with Abraham, Isaac, Jacob, and Joseph. He had worked for four hundred years before the giving of the law, always working by grace and mercy in giving to the people.

The law of Moses, the Ten Words on the tablets of stone on Mount Sinai, could not mean a different arrangement: it was not a change. Paul argued that since the law was not given until 430 years later, it could not change the covenant that God would give His blessing in response to faith. The idea which came up later and which was current at the time Jesus was on earth, that the law was a different way to gain the blessing of God, was a mistaken idea. Paul understood how the Ten Commandments could help a man come to faith; but just now he is arguing that the Ten Words, or the Ten Commandments, are not a departure from the original promise of God; "that this should make the promise of none effect," as if a person now could earn the blessing of God. Paul points out that the law "cannot disannul, that it should make the promise of none effect"; which would be the case if a person were now going to earn it. This brings out the general idea that the original purpose of God, His all-time eternal purpose, was that man will be blessed by the grace of God, the goodwill of God; and the believer is to receive it by faith. It was never intended that any man work for blessing from God; the blessing is a gift from God.

17

THE GIFT
OF ETERNAL LIFE
(3:18-20)

Do you realize the difference in receiving heaven as a gift and in receiving it as wages you have earned?

Salvation is free. Christians rejoice to say that eternal life is a gift. "For by grace are ye saved through faith; and that not of yourselves: it is the gift of God: not of works, lest any man should boast" (Eph. 2:8-9). So often this seems so well understood as to be almost unimportant. This may be because, generally speaking, Christians really are not directly involved in salvation or in eternal life. Perhaps the real reason why it doesn't seem to matter much whether a person has it as a gift or works for it, is the fact that the individual does not have it anyway. For instance, what difference would it make to a person whether peace of mind and heart was a gift of God or the result of personal effort if that person does not have peace anyway?

But to Paul, all of this was very important; and in the Book of Galatians he argues about it over and over again, because this shows the nature of the gospel. He was anxious that these Christians in Galatia should remember that everything that pertained to their spiritual experience came to them originally as a gift, because that meant two things. In the first place, if salvation comes as a gift, a person can count on it being complete, total, and adequate. In the second place, when it is recognized as a gift, it will incline the Christian to be thankful and grateful because of what has been done for him. That is good for one's spirit. To be thankful and grateful for what has been done, and to be expectant because everything has been done that one will ever need, is strengthening to the spiritual life. And this is what Paul wants the Christians to have. If the benefits of salvation were something a person earned, he would be forever on edge lest he did not do enough, or he would be proud because he thinks he has done enough. In the whole Book of Galatians the apostle is arguing that the gospel he preached is that God will freely give everything needed for salvation. This truth is so important that Paul was definitely opposed to any other kind of teaching. Some men were teaching in that area that the Christian gets benefits from God because he keeps rules and regulations. Paul judged this would harm the spiritual experience of the Christians if they heard such ideas. Paul undertook to show that giving by grace has always been God's method; it is not something that has come up after other ways had failed. God always had in mind that man should respond to His will by His grace; which is to say that God would help man to obey Him by inwardly moving him to do so by His grace.

The Galatians were beginning to revert back to Jewish regulations in seeking to serve God. Paul is arguing that to turn back to works as the ground for growth and for stature as a Christian, is actually to forsake the true ways of God in Christ Jesus. "For if the inheritance be of the law, it is no more of promise: but God gave it to Abraham by promise" (3:18). Here Paul is reminding all that logically speaking, if the inheritance or the benefits they have in the gospel were something they had worked for, then it would be no more of promise. It would not be something that God would give. "But God gave it to Abraham by promise." Paul uses Scripture about Abraham to show that the inheritance is essentially a gift, bestowed by God in line with His promises.

The alternative would be to seek the blessing of God as wages, as something one had earned. But Paul reminds the Galatians that God's blessing had been given to Abraham by grace. Paul raises a logical question, "Wherefore then serveth the law?" If the law is not going to help man get right with God, why were the rules and regulations ever brought in? Paul answers his own question: "It was added because of transgressions, till the seed should come to whom the promise was made; and it was ordained by angels in the hand of a mediator" (3:19). He was afraid Christians would turn to the law for the rules by which they could earn the blessing of God. This would be a mistake; this would be an error on their part.

Yet the law was set forth in Scripture; the Ten Words were given. Then why was it there? Paul says it was put there to keep people from trying to please God by their own strength—by doing just the best they knew how. Paul shows the promise to Abraham would eventually be fulfilled in Christ, when the seed would come to whom the promise was made. The promise to Abraham that God would be with him and bless him and keep him would be fulfilled in the seed of Abraham which was Christ, none other than Jesus of Nazareth. The promise was that God's blessing would forever be with His Son, with the Christ, who would obey perfectly. The children of Abraham—those who believed as Abraham did—would enjoy the benefits of the grace of God which God intended to give to them, because of "the seed of Abraham" who would eventually fulfill the law of God. The children of Abraham in their human nature, in the flesh, would be unable to obey the will of God perfectly even if they wanted to. And they would want to because of what God had done for them.

The Scriptural record shows that the children of Israel had been slaves in Egypt. They came out of Egypt because God called them. They had faith, and they rejoiced when they came out of Egypt. When they came through the Red Sea they sang the song of Moses and of Miriam. They sang it with great joy: they had been set free. They traveled in the desert with the cloud by day and the pillar of fire by night, were fed with the manna every morning, and drank of that Rock which followed them, which was Christ. With all these benefits and blessings around them, these people would naturally have wanted to do the will of God. But they were human; and because they were just human in their own strength, they were not able to do the will of God. They faltered and they failed. So rules and regulations were given. The Ten Words were set out to guide these willing people in the way in which God would want them to go, that they might be blessed.

The truth can be seen when thinking of a young woman who is to be married. As a bride she would want to keep house and to cook. Just because she wants to prepare meals for her husband does not mean she can. She may not know how to cook; so someone gives her a cookbook in order that she can learn how to cook. The cookbook does not make her a bride. But being a bride, she would want to cook; so she uses the cookbook. Now the law of Moses was like a cookbook, given to the children of Israel to show them how to do the will of God.

Later in the history of Israel, this meaning was changed by the people who developed a different view. They seemed to accept the idea that if they kept the law they would belong to God. This would be a good deal like saying that if a girl learned how to cook, then she would be married. Of course that would not be true. Keeping house well would not result in the woman being a bride. When the Seed of Abraham would come, then the blessing would be given to Him because of His righteous performance. So until Christ came, the law showed what righteous living was; and these people would be helped by it. Read verse 20: "Now a mediator is not a mediator of one, but God is one." The law dealing with sin needed to be kept, and this law needed to be taught by a priest because the real Seed had not yet appeared. When Jesus of Nazareth came, who was the Seed of Abraham, He did these things in Himself. He did not need anybody to teach Him. Because the Christian is in Christ, the Holy Spirit will lead the believer, who will not need anyone else to teach him what to do.

18

SALVATION IS
FOR THEM THAT BELIEVE
(3:21-22)

Do you realize that no one is ever blessed because he keeps the rules by his own efforts?

Paul continues to show that the gospel of Jesus Christ is that God will bless the believer out of His own grace and mercy because He wants to. God provides salvation, and it comes from Him as a gift. Paul particularly presses this point because error was being taught in the community; something false was being spread around. If it had happened in our day, it could have been said that the Sunday school teachers were teaching something that wasn't true to Scripture. They were saying that a person is blessed if he keeps rules and regulations. Paul had taught a person will be blessed because Christ Jesus died for him and he has put his trust in God. God will bless the believer at the very beginning of his experience. Then he should live in obedience to God because God is moving him to live that way.

Paul emphasizes that salvation comes to the believer by the grace of God only because of his faith in Jesus Christ. This cannot be said too often. God makes His grace available to those who are in Christ Jesus. Would this mean that the Ten Commandments which describe what ought to be done to please God are in opposition to the grace of God? Not at all! There is nothing wrong with the operation of the law, so far as the Ten Commandments are concerned. Paul would say that the law is holy, just, and good. But he would admit at once, as in the seventh chapter of Romans, that the reason why the law doesn't work is the weakness in man. The law tells man what to do, but men are not good enough to do it. What the law requires is right and good, but it is after all only a directive; it is a sign that says "go this way." But what if a person doesn't want to go that way? Or what if a person does want to go that way and finds he cannot? This is the problem that the law faces. There is nothing wrong with saying that God will guide you: "This is the way. Walk ye in it!" That could be quite true, and it would be the way to blessing; but sinners in themselves do not have the disposition or the strength to walk that way.

"Is the law then against the promises of God? God forbid: for if there had been a law given which could have given life, verily righteousness should have been by the law" (3:21). Paul goes on to say, if it had been possible for man to obey, there would have been guidance given in the law that could have led a person into life. Certainly this would have been the quickest way to get it done. But Scripture reveals plainly, as in the latter part of Romans 5, that all men are born in sin; and because they are born in sin and are sinful, they cannot keep the law of God. Their own native natures are carnal and so they are not minded to obey God, even if they would know what His will was. If ever any man is to be blessed of God, he must, in the terms of the gospel, "believe in Jesus Christ."

Jesus of Nazareth was the incarnate Son of God. He obeyed the will of His Father perfectly. He kept the law in every detail, and thus He received the blessing promised to Abraham. Something very profound occurs when a man believes in Jesus Christ. Somehow by God's great power, the individual believer in the Lord Jesus Christ is, in the terms of Paul, "grafted into Christ," as if you took a branch off one tree and grafted it into another fruit tree. In another place Paul says that believers are "adopted as the children of God." The implication is that when a man believes in the Lord Jesus Christ, he becomes one of God's own.

The Holy Spirit, sent into the heart of the believer, takes the things of Christ and shows them to the believer in such a way that they affect his attitudes and actions. Paul writes to the Ephesians that he prays for them, "that Christ may dwell in your hearts by faith." When Christ comes to dwell in the heart He will move the Christian to obey God. He is not merely an honored guest. He comes into the heart as Lord. He comes to govern. When the Christian has the Lord Jesus Christ within his heart, He is the "governor that shall rule my people, Israel." When a soul receives Jesus Christ as Savior and Lord, he will be guided by Him. He shows the believer how to live inwardly. It is by the Holy Spirit's motivation that the will of the Lord is activated in the life of the Christian.

The Christian wants to do God's will, to walk in His way. This is the result of the indwelling Holy Spirit showing the things of Christ and activating the will of the Lord Jesus Christ, who does all things to please His Father. If a person receives Jesus Christ into his heart, he is not just receiving a principle or a goal toward which he is going to work. He receives into his heart One who will live His life in him. This Christ who is received by believing the gospel is already mature and obedient; and when the believer yields himself to His lordship, he will be guided along the ways of Christ and in the way of obedience as one who is of full-grown stature, doing the will of God.

The believer begins by confessing his sins. Christ will then deliver him from his sins. When a person receives Christ as his Savior, Christ comes into the heart and delivers the soul from guilt. He cleanses from sin because He is saving the soul. When a person believes in the Lord Jesus Christ as Savior, he receives from God the Holy Spirit. Taking the things of Christ, the Holy Spirit will actually guide the believer, so he will be obeying the inward guidance of God.

When one takes the Word of God as it is set forth in Scripture, he will come to know the will of God. As a person comes to know the will of God, he can be inclined to walk in the ways of God. Since there is no man that does not sin, such obedience to God is not possible for anybody in the flesh; therefore a person must be born again. When any person receives Jesus Christ as Lord, God regenerates that person. There will be a new creature in him: a new spirit within him. This new creature within the believer responds to the presence of the Lord Jesus Christ, and being moved by His Holy Spirit is activated in his own response into the will of God by the living Lord Jesus Christ. That is why it must be said that salvation is only for those who believe. Salvation is available to anyone: "Whosoever will may come"; but the only persons who come are the people who receive it.

Since Jesus Christ is the Way, the Truth, and the Life, Peter could say, "There is no other name under heaven, given among men, whereby we must be saved." Salvation is provided for those who believe in the Lord Jesus Christ. Thus it is written in Galatians 3:22, "that the promise by faith of Jesus Christ might be given to them that believe." This is the great promise of God in Christ Jesus.

19

THE LAW WAS
OUR SCHOOLMASTER
(3:23-25)

Do you realize that knowing right and wrong will lead you to Christ?

Salvation is by faith in Jesus Christ. It is not a matter of being right or wrong in order to qualify for the blessing of God. No man always does right, and yet all need to have blessing from God. The gospel tells all men that this is available through Jesus Christ the Lord. In Galatians 3:23-25 the truth is openly declared that while the keeping of the law does not make a man just in the sight of God, it does prepare one to receive and understand the things of Christ.

A person may realize the reality of God and acknowledge the truth of His law, but not understand the operation of the grace of God in Christ Jesus. Actually, everyone is subject to the law of God. A man does not have to be a Christian for that; "for whatsoever a man soweth, that shall he also reap" (6:7). It happens to everyone that if a man does what is right in the sight of God, he will be blessed; but if a man does what is wrong in the sight of God, he will be cursed. This was indicated in the Ten Commandments. There is no one living who is not responsible to live in the sight of God according to the Ten Commandments. "Thou shalt not kill" is true all the way across the board. "Thou shalt not steal" is always true. It is incumbent on all men to do right in the sight of God. Each man is responsible to God for the deeds done in the body. The fact is that there is no man living that does not sin.

> But before faith came, we were kept under the law, shut up unto the faith which should afterwards be revealed. Wherefore the law was our schoolmaster to bring us unto Christ, that we might be justified by faith. But after that faith is come, we are no longer under a schoolmaster.—3:23-25

The law is like a schoolmaster to bring men to Christ. The law teaches men righteousness. If a person goes by the law, he will find out what is right and what is wrong in the sight of God. The law teaches what sin is. Any violation or transgression of the law is a sin in the sight of God. And the law prepares men for judgment. So if a person has a knowledge of the law, if he holds up the law as a mirror, and looks into the Ten Commandments as they are set forth in Scripture, he will see for himself that he is a sinner. And he will know, "the soul that sins, it shall die." Now he can realize that he is doomed in the sight of God. This will prepare him to understand the importance of and the need for salvation.

At this point the gospel presents the Lord Jesus Christ. He is the Savior. He came to save sinners. He paid the penalty for yesterday and today, and for all the tomorrows that ever will be. "Though your sins be as scarlet, they shall be as white as snow; though they be red like crimson, they shall be as wool" (Isa. 1:18). This is wonderfully true. But there is more to the gospel than just this forgiveness of sin. The salvation that is in Christ includes not only the forgiveness of sin, but it also includes from God an inward grace that comes in the Person of the Lord Jesus Christ. When a believer realizes that in himself he is a sinner, and in his own conduct and performance he has done wrong and has failed, then in Christ Jesus he can receive the fullness of life. He can actually be saved if he will just receive Christ. And if he responds in faith to the grace that is in Christ Jesus, God will bring salvation into him as it is seen in Christ.

The believer who is once in Christ no longer needs the law. The law told him what to do and what not to do. When now he responds to Christ, so that He is ruling in the soul, the Christian has an inward guidance that comes from the Lord. Scripture reveals about God that He will write His law on the heart of the believer. He will put His Spirit within the Christian so that he will be inwardly led.

Until a person has Christ Jesus in the heart, he needs the law to define outwardly what is right and what is wrong. This is the meaning of the statement: "The law is a schoolmaster to bring us to Christ." When the law tells a person, "Do right . . . avoid wrong," he simply cannot do that unless he has been born again. But after he has been born again, he has a new nature and is given the Holy Spirit. This person can now realize that "the law was our school-master to bring us to Christ" because the law showed him what was right and wrong, showed him that he was wrong, and then showed him that by believing in Christ Jesus he could be forgiven, and that God would work in him "to will and to do of his good pleasure."

"But after that faith is come, we are no longer under a school-master" (3:25). When once a person has received Christ, has been born again, and has received the Holy Spirit he need not go by any external signs as to what is right or what is wrong. He will have that guidance in his own heart. Knowing this, a person would be wise to receive Jesus Christ, who will save the soul.

20

"YE ARE ALL ONE IN CHRIST JESUS"
(3:26-28)

Did you know that the believers in Christ Jesus are all the children of God?

It is the glory of the gospel of the Lord Jesus Christ to offer the grace of God as a free gift to all men—"whosoever will." Scripture emphasizes that God is no respecter of persons. Just because the invitation "Come unto me" is so unrestricted, so open to all, it may be quite natural that some unsound inferences may be assumed on the basis of this. For instance, an example would be that it is not true to say all men are alike in the sight of God. It is certainly obvious they are not alike because there are differences that can be seen. And God must see more differences than are obvious to men. It is true that all men have an equal opportunity before God. God is no respecter of persons in that He does not give the good man more sunlight than the bad man. He does not let the rain fall on the good man rather than on the bad man. Jesus of Nazareth clearly taught that the sun shines and the rain falls on the good and the bad alike; in this sense God is no respecter of persons. And when He gives the call, "Whosoever will, let him come," He means "whosoever"--anyone—"Whosoever will, let him come." But this does not mean to say that all men are alike, even in the sight of God.

On the basis of the open invitation in the gospel to all men, it is sometimes said that no difference should ever be made between people. But why should such an idea be accepted? Who knows what God sees and what He thinks when He looks at men? Some things have been revealed; for instance, that God is angry with the wicked every day. He is not angry with everyone, but He is angry with the wicked every day. The record is revealed about Jesus of Nazareth that just before He went to the Last Supper, "having loved his own, he loved them to the end"; and so He acted in certain definite ways that were aimed at His own disciples whom "he loved."

It is written in Scripture, "Whom the Lord loveth he chasteneth, and scourgeth every son whom he receiveth" (Heb. 12:6). The very way this is expressed implies that such chastening does not come to everyone. It comes only to those who belong to God. Apparently God will act in line with man's response to Him: "Draw nigh unto the Lord and he will draw nigh unto you" (James 4:8). He will do so for any one person as quickly and readily as for any other person. True! One person who is gentle may come to Him; another who has a strong mind may come to Him. He will accept both! One man who is rich comes to Him; another man who is poor comes to Him. He will accept both! That does not mean to say that the rich man is the same as the poor man. It does not say that the strong man is the

80

same as the weak man. It does say God gives an equal opportunity to each one. It is also true that He will never open the door for those who are proud, nor for those who disobey Him. "God resisteth the proud, but giveth grace unto the humble" (James 4:6). In God's eye there is a difference between proud people and humble people.

Paul tells the Galatians: "For ye are all the children of God by faith in Christ Jesus. For as many of you as have been baptized into Christ have put on Christ" (3:26-27). Whom does Paul mean when he says "ye"? To say this means the whole world is to take it entirely out of its context. To whom was the Book of Galatians written? To the churches in Galatia? Exactly! It was the Christians in the church at Galatia who were "all the children of God." It is those who believe, who are in the church of the Lord Jesus Christ, of whom this is true: "You are all the children of God by faith in Christ Jesus." Christians are not the children of God by birth; they are the children of God inasmuch as they have faith in Jesus Christ. God wants everybody to be saved—that is true! God is "not willing that any should perish but that all should come to repentance" (II Peter 3:9). But when Scripture uses the word *Father* it means God is the Father of those whom He has begotten. "No man knoweth the Father save the Son, and he to whomsoever the Son shall reveal him" (Matt. 11:27). All men in some fashion know something about God. "The heavens declare the glory of God; and the firmament showeth his handiwork. Day unto day uttereth speech, and night unto night showeth knowledge" (Ps. 19:1-2). That is true all around the world, and all men can see God as almighty, and God as all-powerful, and God as all-wise, and God as sovereign of all the earth, without knowing anything about Jesus of Nazareth. But never in Scripture would it be found that anyone can know God as Father until he has seen God in Jesus of Nazareth.

The word "baptized" (3:27) seems to refer to the spiritual reality of which the ceremony of baptism is the outward sign. This would be a matter of entering into spiritual relationship with Christ. This happens when a believer openly receives Jesus Christ and confesses Him as Savior, when he commits himself to Him, when he definitely yields himself to Him.

"There is neither Jew nor Greek, there is neither bond nor free, there is neither male nor female: for ye are all one in Christ Jesus" (3:28). One should note very, very carefully why Paul uses the word "Jew" and why he uses the word "Greek." In what sense would it be true that "there is neither Jew nor Greek"? In the sense that Christians are all one; believers in Christ Jesus are one in unity. Insofar as they have put on Christ, it is "Christ in you, the hope of glory." Because they are all in Christ, they are all one. "There is neither bond nor free." The very fact Paul speaks of slaves and of masters indicates that in that society there were those classes of men. But in Christ, believers are neither slaves nor masters. This truth can be seen even more clearly when Scripture notes that "there is neither male nor female." Of course in human society there are men and women, but in Christ Jesus there is no such difference. A simple way of putting this clearly would be to say that while it is true that there is neither Jew nor Greek, neither bond nor free, neither male nor female *in Christ Jesus,* it is also very true that there are Jew and Greek in Galatia; there are bond and free in Galatia, and there are male and female in Galatia. In the communities where Christians live, in the world where believers live, human differences and distinctions will be found. But in Christ Jesus, so far as persons belong to Him, and insofar as He rules in their hearts, there is no difference. They are all one, all who are in Christ Jesus.

21

THE HEIR MUST
GO TO SCHOOL
(3:29—4:2)

Do you realize that Christians must keep the commandments like anybody else?

Being a Christian does not mean that a person has special privilege before God as to right and wrong. There is no doubt that becoming a believer opens the way to great benefits, but that does not mean that a person will be excused from the obligation to do what is right and to avoid what is wrong. The believer may have been poor and in debt before he came to Christ, and when he accepted Christ he became rich; but now that he is rich he will have to pay his bills just as he needed to do when he was poor and in debt.

"And if ye be Christ's, then are ye Abraham's seed, and heirs according to the promise" (3:29). No one born in the flesh as such belongs to Christ. In other words, "born in the flesh" does not mean that a person belongs to Christ. Being a child of Adam is not being a child of God. "But as many as received him, to them gave he power to become the sons of God, even to them that believe on his name" (John 1:12). Christ gave them power to become something they were not. When a person becomes a Christian by faith in Jesus Christ, he becomes one of the seed of Abraham. He becomes an adopted child of God, and as such he is suddenly as rich as his heavenly Father is rich. Before the believer was a Christian, in himself as a human being, he was poor, blind, naked, doomed. When he became a Christian and received Christ Jesus as his Savior, God received him as His son; and thus he is now in line to receive benefits because he belongs to One who is rich.

Being Abraham's seed puts the believer in line to receive the promises of Abraham. The promise is "to thee and to thy seed," and he is one of "the seed." He has become an heir of the promises of God. He inherits what was given to Abraham according to the promise, "and to thy seed." But this change in his status does not give him license to do as he pleases. The law of God is universal and eternal. The Lord Jesus Christ when He was here on earth kept the law of God. He made it a point to say plainly, "I come not to destroy the law, but to fulfill it." And what was true for Him is true for all Christians. Thus the soul living in Christ will honor and obey that law. If Christ is in the heart, He will move the man now to do as He personally did when He was here on earth. He could say, "I do all things to please my Father." When His Spirit is in the believer, and he is being moved by Him as he lives, it will be the desire of the believer to keep the law of God. He will try to do all things to please his Father.

When a person becomes a Christian, there is a sense in which he is as a "newborn babe." Every believer begins as a babe in Christ. When I became a Christian I was a young man. I had developed certain habits, ideas, and values. But when I became a Christian, that night when I realized that Jesus Christ died for me, although in that one blinding flash I came to believe in Him, my heart was changed. I saw things differently, but all my human nature and my human personality was as it was. I was myself. I had received Jesus Christ, but I had all the flesh in me that had been there before. That flesh had its own way of doing things, and I still had it to handle.

Consider a girl who accepts a proposal for marriage. She has been keeping company with some young man, and eventually he asks her to become his wife. She accepts. Now being his wife, she will have to cook, won't she? Would we say that because she accepted him last night and became engaged to marry him, that this morning she is a full-fledged cook? Hardly. She must learn how to cook, how to keep house. Perhaps she knows nothing about housekeeping; but because she loves him, she will certainly want to do it well. So she begins to learn, even though she is a child in these things. She may be just a beginner in these things, but she begins to learn.

So it is with becoming a Christian and serving the Lord. Accepting Jesus Christ brings the believer into the family of God as an heir. But when he comes into the presence of God, he still has his flesh. As long as his flesh has not been crucified, as long as it has not been mortified, as long as his human flesh has not been put to death, he is actually carnal. He is a babe, but by the grace of God he can learn to grow.

> And I, brethren, could not speak unto you as unto spiritual, but as unto carnal, even as unto babes in Christ. I have fed you with milk, and not with meat: for hitherto ye were not able to bear it, neither yet now are ye able. For ye are yet carnal: for whereas there is among you envying, and strife, and divisions, are ye not carnal, and walk as men?—I Cor. 3:1-3

PART SIX

THE REDEEMER

(4:3-31)

22

GOD SENT FORTH
HIS SON TO REDEEM
(4:3-5)

Have you understood that Christ Jesus came not to show men what
to do but to redeem?

At the moment a person accepts Jesus Christ and thereby becomes a Christian, he is still in the flesh. He is still a human being.
Every person starts out in life as a human being. He is born into this
world from human parents, as a child of Adam. Paul calls this
inheritance from his biological parents "the flesh"—neither good nor
bad, but susceptible to sin. Just being alive means in the language of
the New Testament that a person is in the flesh and therefore an
unforgiven sinner. Adam was a sinner, and all that are born of him
are sinners; and so each believer was once an unforgiven sinner. He
would naturally want to be what he wanted to be, and that is sinful.
But it is to him as a sinner that Christ Jesus came to save. "God
commendeth his love toward us, in that, while we were yet sinners,
Christ died for us" (Rom. 5:8). Through the Holy Spirit He now
offers the gospel which will redeem man from his sinfulness.

John the Baptist brought this message in his preaching, "Repent
ye; for the kingdom of heaven is at hand" (Matt. 3:2). Repentance is
the attitude a person takes toward himself as a sinner, now that the
opportunity of deliverance is here. When a person receives Jesus
Christ as his Savior, he becomes a child of God. Paul would say the
believer is adopted into the family of God. This means specifically
for the believer that he is forgiven. He is pardoned. He is now "at

one" with God. All this is true for the believer in Christ Jesus, and it is activated in him by the Holy Spirit. God begins to deal with him on this basis, because on this basis as a believer in Christ he is an heir of God, a joint-heir with Jesus Christ. When a person believes in the Lord Jesus Christ, in the sight of God he becomes one with Him; and He is now one with him.

Since the Lord Jesus Christ obeyed the Father perfectly, and the Father is pleased with Him—"This is my beloved Son, in whom I am well pleased"—the Father's attitude is to bless the believer and to bless those who belong to Him. Christ Jesus in His grace has called him to come. As he is in himself, he is not fit nor good nor strong; but he has heard the call and he has come to Christ and put his trust in Him. So as surely as he does that, Almighty God begins to deal with him as though he belonged to Christ. God begins to deal with him because he is now in Christ and is an heir of God, but he still has his flesh. He still has his first human nature, and from this he must be delivered. As a newborn babe in Christ, when he received Christ Jesus as his Savior, his flesh, which he got from his parents, from the community in which he was reared, from the culture and the society in which he lives, is still alive and strong and active. As such, it must be kept under the law because this flesh is still responsible to obey: "thou shalt not kill; thou shalt not steal; thou shalt not covet." The law is still true so far as his flesh is concerned. And he still has the disposition to do these things, for in spite of the law of God there is no man that does not sin. Christ Jesus came to die, to redeem him from the flesh; and He has a way of doing it.

Christ Jesus can set the believer free from his flesh by a very simple procedure. Paul talked about this in Romans 7, when he pointed out the conditions under which a woman can be set free from her husband. A woman who is married to her husband is not free to marry anybody else as long as her husband lives; but when her husband dies, the woman is free. The death of the husband will liberate her and she may marry whom she chooses in the Lord. The apostle Paul used that illustration to show what happens with a person spiritually speaking when the flesh dies, because it is the flesh that keeps a person under the law. In the flesh he is liable to sin. The flesh in itself is sinful; and even though the law restrains him, he has the disposition to want to do selfishly the things that he is pleased to do in the flesh. But God has a way of delivering him from the flesh. That way is to have the flesh die. When the flesh dies, and the believer dies in the flesh, God will raise him from the dead in the newness of life. That new thing that He raises from the dead will not be in the flesh. It will be in the spirit that is in Christ Jesus; and this spirit is minded to do the will of God. This is God's way of setting the believer free. God wants the flesh to die, so that the believer will be free. When the flesh dies, when the human spirit is counted as dead, then the believer is free from temptation and from all personal considerations, because you cannot tempt a dead man. In this way he is actually set free. Someone might say, "But, when you are dead, you are dead." But God can raise the dead; and so when the believer dies in the flesh and by that is set free from the temptations and the ideas of sin, and is raised from the dead in the newness of life, he can live on in Christ Jesus.

The apostle Paul told the Galatians: "I am crucified with Christ: nevertheless I live; yet not I, but Christ liveth in me" (2:20). This is the sense in which believers are redeemed. "Even so we, when we were children, were in bondage under the elements of the world" (4:3). When Paul speaks of children he means that believers were beginners; they were still immature. First, the believer was born in the flesh; then he was born again in the spirit. The old man is older, bigger, and stronger than the new man. The new man is younger, but he has all the power of eternity in him. In this situation he is in bondage because of the flesh. "But when the fulness of the time was come, God sent forth his Son, made of a woman, made under the law, To redeem them that were under the law, that we might receive the adoption of sons" (4:4-5). The Lord Jesus Christ actually came along to do something that would redeem men who were under the law.

What would put any man under the law? His human nature. Why was he under the law? Because his human nature was sinful. He had the disposition to do wrong because he was a child of Adam. When this spiritual event of accepting Christ takes place, he reckons himself dead but alive to Christ Jesus; and he actually looks into the presence of God to live in Him. He can be set free. When he is raised from the dead in the spirit, he can be redeemed. Christ Jesus did this by dying for sinners. And so it is even for us today: Christ Jesus died in His own flesh, that the believer, by faith being a partaker of Christ's death, can count that he is crucified with Christ. Therefore this is the task of faith, "to reckon therefore ourselves indeed to be dead unto sin but alive unto God." This is the sort of thing that Paul is arguing about here; this is all part of delivering believers from this present evil world, which God does through the Lord Jesus Christ.

23

GOD SENT FORTH
HIS SPIRIT INTO BELIEVERS
(4:6-7)

Did you know that the Holy Spirit is given to produce holiness in a special way?

It is a joy to say that the gospel is for everybody. The witness to Jesus Christ can stand up before the whole world and say anybody can come. The gospel is free. Everyone has the privilege. Anybody can come, but not everybody will come. Anyone can come to God, but one cannot come any way. One must come in God's way. To say that Christ Jesus died for all is not to say that all are now saved. Sadly it must be admitted that not everybody will be saved. "Whosoever believeth in him shall not perish but have everlasting life" is wonderfully true, but there are some who do not believe in Him. It is believing in Him, trusting in Him, committing oneself to His promise, that is the saving principle. "But as many as received him, to them gave he power to become the sons of God" (John 1:12).

Anyone can, but not everyone will. This is also seen in the truth about the Holy Spirit of God.

> And because ye are sons, God hath sent forth the Spirit of his Son into your hearts, crying, Abba, Father. Wherefore thou art no more a servant, but a son; and if a son, then an heir of God through Christ.—4:6-7

Why should it be said that the Holy Spirit was put into the heart of every believer, unless we say that the Lord Jesus Christ died for every sinner? But this is true. It can be said that the Lord Jesus Christ Christ died for every sinner, but it must be said at once that not everybody is saved. So it can be said that the Holy Spirit was given to every believer, but it doesn't follow that every believer has received the Holy Spirit. When the fact is emphasized that Jesus Christ died for sinners on Calvary's cross and that whosoever will may come, the preacher is saying, "Come." Then is promised, "Whosoever cometh, he will in no wise cast out." This is wonderfully true. But this is also true: "And because ye are sons, God hath sent forth the Spirit of his Son into your hearts, crying, Abba, Father" (4:6). Almighty God has given the Holy Spirit, but He does not force Him on anyone. The Holy Spirit needs to be received by believers even as the Lord Jesus needs to be received by sinners. Actually, the sinner was urged to receive the Lord Jesus Christ that he might not be destroyed. The sinner was reminded that "the wages of sin is death." He could feel in himself that he had done wrong and he knew that he would be destroyed. The preacher is saying to this man who is facing destruction: "You can be saved from destruction. You can actually be delivered from this. Believe on the Lord Jesus Christ and you will be saved."

It could be said to Christians that if they would receive the Holy Spirit of God, then they would be blessed. The appeal to Christians is not concerned with sin. Sin is forgiven because they believe in the Lord Jesus Christ. But the emphasis is on service. The emphasis is on responding to God, on doing the will of God. A person who has been saved by the grace of the Lord Jesus Christ and has been washed by the blood of the Lamb and realizes that he is free because Christ Jesus died for him, will find in himself a gratitude toward God.

There will be in him a readiness to say, "Here am I, send me": a willingness to have God tell him what to do. Now to such a person, wanting to do the will of God, looking forward and wanting to serve God, comes the great truth that God has given him the Holy Spirit.

A Christian who is looking ahead, wanting to please God, wanting to serve God, could receive the Holy Spirit into his heart and mind, and let the Holy Spirit guide him. It happens in just the same way as the sinner who wants to be saved, who doesn't want to go to hell, who wants to go to heaven, can receive Jesus Christ. The sinner is promised that if he will receive the Lord Jesus Christ as Savior, God will not destroy him; but God will save him to eternal life. To the person who is a Christian, who knows the Lord and who belongs to God, the promise is given: "Do you want to serve Him? Do you want to be fruitful? Would you like to be well pleasing in the sight of God? Then receive the Holy Spirit of God." The Holy Spirit is given to the believer to enable him to walk in the ways of God. The Holy Spirit needs to be received by believers even as the Lord Jesus Christ needs to be received by sinners.

"Wherefore thou art no more a servant, but a son; and if a son, then an heir of God through Christ" (4:7). A servant is one who does what he is told. But a son is one who wants to be well pleasing to his father, who belongs to his father. He is part of the whole family, so everything about it belongs to him. He is an heir of his father and a joint-heir with the other children in the family, so everything that is done for the benefit of the family is really done for the benefit of this son. Believers are to be considered as sons; in a very real way this is how they can be seen. It is the indwelling of the Holy Spirit that makes the difference. As long as a person is under the command of the law, he is as a servant. But when he is doing what he is doing because he wants to be well pleasing, because he belongs, he is acting like a son. "And if a son, then an heir." He is an heir of God through Christ, just as he is a child of God.

When the believer lets the Holy Spirit of God operate in him, he will be moved inwardly to talk to the Father, saying, "Abba, Father." He will draw nigh to the Father with words of affection and of close, intimate rejoicing in the Lord, as a child does to the parent. It is because the believer is a son that it is said he is an heir. This is a way of saying that the blessings of the gospel are for such as respond to the Holy Spirit to become the sons of God.

"But when the fulness of the time was come, God sent forth his Son, made of a woman, made under the law, To redeem them that were under the law, that we might receive the adoption of sons" (4:4-5). So believers are saved by the death of the Lord Jesus Christ.

"And because ye are sons, God hath sent forth the Spirit of his Son into your hearts, crying, Abba, Father. Wherefore thou art no more a servant, but a son; and if a son, then an heir of God through Christ" (4:6-7). Paul is emphasizing how much has been done for believers in Christ Jesus, and that this is actually available to them because the Holy Spirit is given to them. Christians need to have the Holy Spirit operative in them, that they may fully receive what is provided for them as the children of God.

24

CHILDREN OF GOD
ARE FREE FROM BONDAGE
(4:8-11)

Do you realize that when a person once becomes a Christian, he is free from rules before God?

Before a person becomes a Christian, it would be natural for him, in trying to order his life in the better way, to do so by certain rules and regulations. He would be attempting to do the whole thing! While he was growing up, his parents taught him: "Do this; don't do that." When he grew older, he would accept goals that nice people have. All of this is human. Society agrees generally what is right and wrong. Folkways and customs are derived from the society in which men live.

But this is not how it goes with a Christian. The apostle Paul has been arguing in the Epistle to the Galatians that being a Christian is a matter of yielding oneself to God, and letting the Holy Spirit show one the will of God. Paul was aware that in Galatia certain persons were teaching that if a person wanted to be saved, he should keep the laws and the regulations which the Jewish people kept. But Paul said, "No, if you want to be a Christian, you must yield to the living Lord and let Him have His way in you. He has given you His Holy Spirit for that very purpose."

> Howbeit then, when ye knew not God, ye did service unto them which by nature are no gods. But now, after that ye have known God, or rather are known of God, how turn ye again to the weak and beggarly elements, whereunto ye desire again to be in bondage? Ye observe days, and months, and times, and years. I am afraid of you, lest I have bestowed upon you labour in vain.—4:8-11

Paul is saying that he is afraid that the Galatian believers do not have the reality of living as Christians, for they are going by rules and regulations instead of going by the inward guidance of the living Lord. Here is a clear description of any person who is not a Christian: "Howbeit then, when ye knew not God, ye did service unto them which by nature are no gods" (4:8). Knowing God is far more than knowing about God. A person can know about God because he reads about Him in a book. He can know about God because he hears somebody talk about Him. *But does he know God?* He could not know Him unless he saw Him face to face, unless he actually confronted Him and had dealings with Him. This is the significance of being a Christian. A person who knows God is a person who understands and appreciates the fact that God in Christ Jesus will actually deliver him. He will put his trust in God, and he will seek to be well pleasing in His sight.

"But now, after that ye have known God, or rather are known of God" (4:9). This is an interesting description of a Christian. A

Christian does know God. He knows Him in Christ Jesus. Paul says more carefully: "or rather are known of God"; that is, when God knows him. To say that God knows the believer means far more than to say He knows who he is, that He knows about him. It means God accepts him. He counts him as His child.

"How turn ye again to the weak and beggarly elements, whereunto ye desire again to be in bondage?" (4:9). The "weak and beggarly elements" refer to the law and rules and regulations. When a person is a Christian and is experiencing "Christ in you," he will be led inwardly. "Thou shalt worship the Lord thy God and him only shalt thou serve." How do parents tell a child that he should worship God? It is quite possible that they will say the child should respect the Lord's Day. He should treat the Sabbath Day differently from other days, and they train the child to do it. It is largely a matter of negative rules. The parents will say, "You must not do this on Sunday, you must not do that on Sunday." But is this real worshiping? Is this really what God wanted when He said, "Thou shalt worship the Lord thy God and him only shalt thou serve"? Worshiping God is from the heart. The Christian really wants to be pleasing in His sight.

Another illustration would be the season of the year that is called Lent. At that time it is the custom to sacrifice, to give up something, to fast. The worshiper will not eat meat, nor go to dances, nor do this or that during Lent. It happens that just before Lent begins, people often celebrate Mardi Gras. This is a time of hilarity and indulgence. Then immediately after Lent is over the custom is to have a big dance or something of that nature. Is all this really a matter of worshiping God?

This is what Paul is talking about. He writes, "Ye observe days, and months, and times, and years. I am afraid of you, lest I have bestowed upon you labour in vain." God would have in mind that while it is very proper for the believer to keep Sunday as the Lord's Day and it is very proper for him to be careful not to do anything disrespectful to Him, what really counts is the way the believer feels in his heart, the way in which he is drawn to God. So far as the children of God are concerned, it is not a matter of keeping rules and regulations: that is not the important thing. The important thing is that they keep themselves close to the Lord in spirit, and do what is well pleasing in His sight.

25

GENUINE GROWTH
DOES NOT DENY THE PAST
(4:12-20)

Would you think getting a new idea means you must discount the old?

Being a Christian is primarily a matter of belonging to God through a personal commitment to Jesus Christ. It is a good deal like getting married. Marriage is far more real and permanent than any ideas the engaged couple may have cherished. Certainly a girl once married will get new ideas of what it means to be married. These new ideas do not change nor invalidate her marriage vows. The original vows still count. So when a believer in Jesus Christ has once committed himself to God in Christ, he may get new ideas of what spiritual life means, what it means to walk in the Lord. But these new views do not cancel his original commitment.

Paul made a plea for continuation of their good will. "I beseech you, let us remain close together. I haven't taken any offense at what has happened. My heart is right with you; you keep your heart right with me." Then he reminds them. Paul had preached the gospel to them even though he had been afflicted by some weakness or Christians that they still belonged to God, no matter what new views they may have.

Brethren, I beseech you, be as I am; for I am as ye are: ye have not injured me at all. Ye know how through infirmity of the flesh I preached the gospel unto you at the first. And my temptation which was in my flesh ye despised not, nor rejected; but received me as an angel of God, even as Christ Jesus.—4:12-14

Paul made a plea for continuation of their good will. "I beg you, let us remain close together. I haven't taken any offense at what has happened. My heart is right with you; you keep your heart right with me." Then he reminds them. Paul had preached the gospel to them even though he had been afflicted by some weakness or sickness or disease. But in spite of that they did not hold it against him that he was a sick man. They had received him as "an angel of God, even as Christ Jesus." They had honored him as if he was a true messenger from God. They even honored him as though he was the Lord Jesus Christ Himself. Paul then presses his point home. "Where is then the blessedness ye spake of?" What happened to the happy joyful feeling that you had; "For I bear you record, that, if it had been possible, ye would have plucked out your own eyes, and have given them to me." Paul reminds them—and he could testify to the whole world—that in those days when he was with the Galatians, they were one hundred percent on his side. They would have done anything to help him out. Paul had no objection to these Christians being interested in other things, as long as the things were good.

"My little children, of whom I travail in birth again until Christ be formed in you" (4:19). This would indicate that when they at first were becoming Christians, when Paul was preaching as an evangelist, he actually experienced (as we would say) birth pangs in trying to bring these people to faith. He was actually struggling in his own spirit, agonizing that they might come to faith. Now he finds himself doing the same thing, just as if he was having labor pains all over again, because they seemed to be off on the wrong track. "Until Christ be formed in you": until you get the real truth and under-standing of the Lord Jesus Christ. It will be helpful to read this passage in the New Testament in Modern English as translated by J. B. Phillips:

I do beg you to follow me here, my brothers. I am a man like yourselves, and I have nothing against you personally.

You know how handicapped I was by illness when I first preached the Gospel to you. You didn't shrink from me or let yourselves be revolted at the disease which was such a trial to me. No, you welcomed me as though I were an angel of God, or even as though I were Jesus Christ Himself! What has happened to that fine spirit of yours? I guarantee that in those days you would, if you could, have plucked out your eyes and given them to me. Have I now become your enemy because I continue to tell you the same truth? Oh, I know how keen these men are to win you over, but can't you see that it is for their own ends? They would like to see you and me separated altogether, and have you all to themselves. Don't think I'm jealous—it is a grand thing that men should be keen to win you, whether I'm there or not, provided it is for the truth. Oh, my dear children, I feel the pangs of childbirth all over again till Christ be formed within you, and how I long to be with you now! Perhaps I could then alter my tone to suit your mood. As it is, I honestly don't know how to deal with you.

This is a good deal like a discussion that goes on between two people who have been friends, and have been close to each other, but now one of them does not understand the change in the other person's attitude.

This passage can be helpful since it is an example of what happens any time new ideas spread in the church. When people who have been brought up in the gospel to understand it a certain way begin to listen to new ideas, they draw away from the very preachers and teachers that gave them the gospel that they had. That in itself can make them realize that it could be they that are changing, and they should give very serious thought as to whether or not they are changing in a good direction.

26

THE TWO COVENANTS
(4:21-27)

Do you have a clear picture that becoming a Christian is a choice between two different ways of seeking the blessing of God?

Becoming a Christian is something that a person does consciously. The gospel comes as a "call"; it comes to the attention of the sinner; it is something that he must hear; it is something to which he must respond. Choice is involved. He will come or he won't come. He will respond, or he will refuse to respond. Either he will come to God, or he will not come to God.

What happens when a man becomes a Christian is very much like what happens between two young people who have been dating for a period of time. Then comes a day when there is discussion of marriage, and a proposal is made. Often there is amusing confusion in the memories of married couples when they try to recall when and how the proposal took place. Neither may remember what was said, but there is no doubt this event did take place. Accepting Christ is probably a good deal like that. There could very well be some obscurity in one's memory as to just exactly what was happening in the consciousness and exactly what he was thinking at the time, but it can be remembered on that day the Lord was dealing with his soul.

In chapter 4:21-27 Paul narrows the issue that confronted the Galatians when they became Christians to a simple choice of one of two ways. The Bible talks about being dead or alive. You are "in" or you are "out." You are for or against. "There is a narrow road that leadeth unto life, few there be that find it; there is a wide road that leadeth unto destruction; many there be that go thereat" (Matt. 7:14). Two ways: a narrow road—a wide way. One man built his house on a rock, another man built his house on sand. There is no one else mentioned. Just two ways! In the New Testament we read,

"He that hath the Son, hath life; he that hath not the Son of God hath not life." It is kept as simple as that.

In writing to the Galatians Paul speaks of two covenants. He illustrates this truth by referring to the two sons which Abraham had from two wives. One son was Ishmael, whose mother was Hagar; the other son was Isaac, whose mother was Sarah. There are two different ways of looking to receive blessing from God. One is the right way; the other is the wrong way. The Bible keeps it simple. One way leads to bondage. Paul says that the other one leads to freedom. One of these ways turns to the flesh and leads into death; the other one turns to the Spirit and leads into life. Paul writes:

> Tell me, ye that desire to be under the law, do ye not hear the law? For it is written, that Abraham had two sons, the one by a bondmaid, the other by a freewoman. But he who was of the bondwoman was born after the flesh; but he of the freewoman was by promise.—4:21-23

The bondwoman was Hagar, and the freewoman was Sarah. The child born to Hagar was Ishmael, the child born to Sarah was Isaac. Ishmael was born after the flesh; his birth took place in the natural process of biological generation. Isaac's birth was of promise. God promised Abraham, when he was about a hundred years old and Sarah past the age when women have children, that they would have a child and that this child would be Isaac.

> Which things are an allegory: for these are the two covenants; the one from the mount Sinai, which gendereth to bondage, which is Agar. For this Agar is mount Sinai in Arabia, and answereth to Jerusalem which now is, and is in bondage with her children.—4:24-25

In the time of the apostle Paul the Jewish people were seeking to gain the favor of God by works. They were trying the best they knew how to keep the rules and regulations as outlined by their teachers, with the feeling that if this was done they would be right in the sight of God.

But Jerusalem which is above is free, which is the mother of us all. For it is written, Rejoice, thou barren that bearest not; break forth and cry, thou that travailest not: for the desolate hath many more children than she which hath a husband.—4:26-27

The truth of the matter is that the person who tries to be right in the sight of God by what he does, gets deeper into bondage. He wants to deal with God on the basis of his actions but finds that his actions are not acceptable in God's sight. The other way is to receive from God as a gift that which God is willing to give, and that is the "Jerusalem that now is" in heaven. It is real, spiritual; and it will lead into freedom.

The law is holy, just, and good. There is nothing wrong with the law. But it will not work because the natural man will not keep it. Grace is also holy, just, and good. But grace will work because it is God who does it. So the second way of faith would eventually be the greater in all of the things that pertain to heaven. And this is what Paul is seeking to point out. There are two different ways of receiving benefits. One is to work for them, the other is to receive them as a gift. Paul wanted these Galatian Christians to know that the blessings they needed from God would come to them as a free gift through the Lord Jesus Christ.

27
CHILDREN OF FAITH ARE PERSECUTED
(4:28-31)

If a person were a true Christian, do you think anybody would object?

Becoming a Christian is essentially a personal matter of turning to

God in repentance and accepting Jesus Christ as Savior and Lord. It happens inside one's own soul. It has to do with a man's relationship to his God. It is obvious that after such a person has turned to God to receive Jesus Christ, he will be humble and yielded to God and desire to serve Him.

Take, for instance, a woman in her home: a wife and mother. She has a spiritual experience in which she accepts Christ, and now she is really going to walk with Him. This is a real, personal spiritual experience; now she is humble and kind and patient and gentle. One could expect everybody in her family to be glad about the change in her way of living, but strange to say this is not always the case.

What often happens is similar to the situation when a person has been a member of the church for some time and then suddenly has a profound spiritual experience. This person now really believes in the Lord, and so cares for other people. It could be expected every member in that congregation would be glad. The astonishing truth is that former friends may turn away.

Some years ago a man told of his own personal experience. He had at one time been a Jewish rabbi. Then as a result of personal spiritual experience in connection with the death of his wife, he became interested in spiritualism. He actually attended seances and supposedly received messages from his dead wife. Later, he became interested in Christian Science. Still later in an amazing way he came to know the Lord Jesus Christ personally as his Lord and Savior. He told about the strange things that followed. As long as he had been a rabbi he had free access to the high school auditorium and was a frequent speaker at school affairs. Later on, when he became a Reader in this sect to which I referred, he again had free access to the high school and could share in the program. But when he became an earnest Christian, and now talked with people about being saved, he was no longer allowed to speak in that high school!

Similar consequences can be seen even in preachers. When a preacher comes along with some new view that raises doubts about the Bible or lowers confidence in the Bible, people will tolerate him. He may even be called a progressive thinker. Some will say that now he is really up to date. Unconsciously, as the public reacts in this way, the implication is that if any view is new, it must be better. But in the event a preacher comes who will emphasize that the Bible is the Word of God, it is true exactly as it is written—this minister may actually be unwelcome. He may not be wanted. Other preachers themselves will criticize him. It is not unusual to witness tolerance and permission given to men who handle Scripture as if it was not all true; but at the same time criticism, rejection, and disapproval may be shown to men who honor the Bible as the Word of God. This is an astonishing thing.

Christians may welcome a scholar, looking up to him with appreciation and with esteem, even though he does not even believe the Bible as the Word of God. Such a man may explain all Christian experience on purely natural grounds, giving some psychological explanation for all the phenomena of faith. He may actually take away the things of the living Lord Jesus Christ. At the same time there are well-known institutions, schools, colleges, and churches that have ministers, teachers, and professors who are competent, capable, trained men who believe the Bible is the Word of God. Any time they speak it can be depended that this is what they will teach. They will show people what the gospel means. But often they are not welcomed. Apparently this is not a recent development but has long been true.

> Now we, brethren, as Isaac was, are the children of promise. But as then he that was born after the flesh persecuted him that was born after the Spirit, even so it is now. Nevertheless what saith the scripture? Cast out the bondwoman and her son: for the son of the bondwoman shall not be heir with the son of the freewoman. So then, brethren, we are not children of the bondwoman, but of the free.—4:28-31

So Paul points out that believers in the gospel are the children of promise; they are like Isaac. Christian people live before God in faith. Christian faith is not the result of human effort, nor the result of natural processes. Christian faith is in response to some promise of the living God that was seen in Jesus Christ. All the promises of

God are yea and amen in Christ Jesus; so everything Christian people have comes from Him personally. The spiritual, born-again person actually receives these things from God as He speaks them.

The person who is natural and human finds fault with the spiritual person. He belittles, criticizes, and opposes him. As it was then, when Ishmael made fun of Isaac, so it is even to this day. "Nevertheless what saith the scripture?" Paul points out that what Abraham had to do was to put out Ishmael. He had to send him away. The "son of the bondwoman" refers to such who are after the flesh and who actually criticize those who are after the Spirit. Such natural thinking persons are to be "cast out." "The son of the bondwoman shall not be heir with the son of the freewoman." Apparently both of these types exist side by side. This does not mean they are both right or acceptable to God. Both the wheat and the tares grow in the same field until the harvest, but one will be accepted and the other rejected. Christians are not obligated to keep both the natural and the spiritual in the same fellowship. The person who discusses things about Scripture in a human way is one kind of person, and the person who discusses these things in a spiritual way is another kind of person. These two are not expected to walk together.

PART SEVEN

CHRIST GIVES
FREEDOM

(5:1-12)

28

LIBERTY
IS IN CHRIST
(5:1-2)

Do you realize a Christian could lose something important by starting to live by rules?

Being a Christian is a matter of being delivered from this present evil world. It is being set free from the things of the flesh. Being a Christian means to be pardoned so far as sins are concerned: to be released so far as habits and inward tendencies are concerned. In being a Christian, a person is considered as having died in the flesh. The human nature is crucified with Christ. Believers deny themselves; and having done this, they find that they are no longer given over to sin. They do not have to sin any more. They are alive in the Spirit. They are inwardly motivated by the Holy Spirit of God to do the will of God. And now a very strange thing happens. On the one hand Christians speak of themselves as being bondslaves to Christ. What that language actually means is they are permanently enslaved to Christ Jesus. And yet those are the very people who are free, utterly free. But one has to be careful how he uses this language. The person who is a slave to Christ, being totally yielded and obligated to Him, is free from everything else. He belongs to Christ.

For instance, a young girl who grows up in a certain community goes to high school where she meets many other girls and boys. Then one day this particular girl marries a certain young man. From the moment she marries him she is set free from all social engagements and obligations and relationships with all these other people. There is a sense in which when she commits herself to this one. She is free from all others.

This is what happens when a person becomes a Christian. Paul was anxious that Christians should realize this freedom. Believers are set free, by "being raised in the newness of life" in Christ Jesus.

To place this freedom that they have in Christ Jesus under rules is to stifle it. Rules were designed for the old human nature. When I become a Christian, I have the Ruler in my heart. I do not need a set of instructions; I have the Great Instructor in my soul. I am no longer responsible to keep regulations; I have the Regulator Himself inside me.

This was the problem that developed in Galatia. Paul had preached the gospel of the Lord Jesus Christ to these people and had told them that if they would believe in Him they would be saved; they would belong to God and God would belong to them. They had so believed, and had so received the Lord Jesus Christ and rejoiced in Him. Then preachers coming from Jerusalem began to teach that if they would keep rules, they would be better Christians; that if they would structure their activities according to certain regulations, they would get further. This was saying that they could work their way closer to God. Paul calls this "another gospel," and it bothered him.

Paul's great emphasis was that keeping rules does not enable anyone to come closer to God. Keeping rules did not bring them to God in the first place. Believing in Christ Jesus brought them to God. That was the reconciliation which was worked out when they believed in Jesus Christ.

Earlier in this epistle it was pointed out that the law is a schoolmaster to bring men to Christ. Thus rules and regulations are a fine thing for the unbelieving man, the person who does not know Christ. Any human being in his natural self needs rules and regulations so that he will not go completely into chaos; or as it is said, "go haywire." The natural man needs rules, regulations, fences, and curbs, because his disposition is to go in all directions in random activity. He must put himself under control; and so there are rules and regulations that tell him, "You may not go here; you may not go there; this is my garden; this is my lawn; this is my house; you may not go in here; you may not go in there."

However, when a person becomes a Christian, all this is changed. He no longer has the inward disposition to do as he pleases; he has in him the Person of the Lord Jesus Christ. With His presence within, the believer has forgiveness from God. He has help and guidance from God. Living in Christ, as led by the Holy Spirit in the Person of the Lord Jesus Christ, will increase his spiritual experience.

Paul is emphasizing here that spiritual growth is not by works, but by faith.

> Stand fast therefore in the liberty wherewith Christ hath made us free, and be not entangled again with the yoke of bondage. Behold, I Paul say unto you, that if ye be circumcised, Christ shall profit you nothing.—5:1-2

When Paul says "if ye be circumcised," he means that if the believer accepts Jewish circumcision to help him in his Christian living, "Christ shall profit you nothing." By this Paul means to say that a person will not get any help from the Lord Jesus Christ about living that way. However, if the believer was to yield himself to Christ and let Him work His will in him, he would receive the blessing. If the Christian is seeking to establish his own righteousness, he will be without the grace of God and without the power of His indwelling Holy Spirit. This is a very solemn truth.

When a person becomes a Christian, he believes in the Lord Jesus Christ, is accepted of God, and rejoices in his salvation. In this epistle Paul points out that to develop a list of *do's* and *don'ts* will not build up the believer in spiritual things. Regulations will not draw him nearer to God. One can think of a person who does not do anything that is commonly considered wrong: he does not drink alcoholic beverages, he does not use tobacco, he does not dance, he does not play cards, he does not go to theaters—perhaps he does not do anything. Would this make him a Christian? No; more than this must be expected. Paul explains that if the believer has the Holy Spirit and the living Lord Jesus Christ within him, it will be far more important that he does what the Lord wants him to do, than to try to keep a set of regulations.

29

RIGHTEOUSNESS IS BY FAITH
(5:3-5)

Do you understand that if I am trying to be right by my own efforts, I am actually ignoring what the gospel offers to me?

Becoming a Christian is something a sinner can do because anyone can become a Christian. Eternal life is a gift, and when a sinner accepts Christ it is normal that he will want to start living right. The believer does not earn it; this is very humbling. Human beings would like to earn it. If they could earn salvation they could be proud. It is natural for a man to want to earn things and to achieve his own rightness. It is a humbling thing to stand before God, simply dependent on Him.

Paul reminds the Galatians that they have become Christians by believing in the Lord Jesus Christ, and so points out that they will grow as Christians by believing in the Lord Jesus Christ. You became a Christian freely because God gave salvation to you. You didn't work to become a Christian. Nor are you going to work to become a better, stronger Christian. God will do it for you, as you understand His ways and yield yourself to Him. The people who became Christians, became such by receiving the grace of God as a gift.

In Galatia there were people who were beginning to set up rules for the believers to grow stronger and come nearer to God. You might say, "What about these rules? What were they like?" For example, in worship, some feel they cannot pray unless they pray a formal prayer. I one time knew a very sincere woman who would never pray anything but the Lord's Prayer. She was genuinely sincere. She just really and truly said that when the disciples called on the Lord, "Teach us to pray," He taught them the Lord's Prayer; and that is the only prayer she would offer. And I want to tell you that so far as her Christian life was concerned, she was deeply spiritual. I believe that Almighty God understood her very well, and heard the cry of her heart which she never expressed in words. But I do think she was limiting herself.

The Galatians also had certain religious ceremonies that dealt with food and its preparation, as to whether it was "kosher." Also they had certain procedures, such as washing of hands in a certain way before one ate; and if one did not wash his hands one would be committing a sin. There were rules that forbade eating with Gentiles. This was Jewish custom being brought over into the church, and this is what Paul was resisting.

This is seen today. You will have some Christians who want to attend church, but not too often. These people may be altogether unconscious of the fact that while they were in church their minds and hearts were somewhere else. Sitting there in the congregation they were thinking about where they were going the next day, where they had been the day before, what somebody was wearing, and how They would enjoy this. Their minds could be wool gathering and day dreaming, but they're in church. So when they are through, they feel they have done something because they were in church. Paul saw that this tendency to feel self-satisfied because one did certain things could be detrimental to one's spiritual living. Paul writes in Galatians 5:3, "For I testify again to every man that is circumcised, that he is debtor to do the whole law." That is to say, Paul applied that to every man who accepted Jewish circumcision after he was a Christian. So he was a Christian because he believed in the Lord Jesus Christ. Someone came along and said to him he should have been circumcised the way the Jews were. If he tried to please God by adopting this regulation, "he is a debtor to do the whole law." He has undertaken to obey everything in the law. He should then obey all the rules and regulations.

"Christ is become of no effect unto you, whosoever of you are justified by the law; ye are fallen from grace" (5:4). I know this passage bothers some people, but in context it is not so difficult. If you are going to try and get right with God by rules and regulations, you do not need Christ. He is not specially working in you, and He has become of no effect unto you. How would Christ affect you? He would do it by moving you and guiding you by His will. You in turn would derive your inspiration from a face-to-face relationship with Him. You would personally be conscious of the living Lord Jesus Christ. If He is living His life in you, He will be effecting things in you. It will be "Christ in you, the hope of glory." Now if you are trying to get right with God by keeping rules and regulations, you are not depending on the indwelling Christ. That is the meaning of saying "Christ is become of no effect."

"Ye are fallen from grace" means this: You've stopped depending on the grace of God and have started depending on your own observances, your own regulations. You are not depending on inward strength to do the will of God, but are depending on outward compliance with rules and regulations. This is what Paul is emphasizing.

"For we through the Spirit wait for the hope of righteousness by faith" (5:5). Wait . . . the Christian procedure is to be led! "We through the Spirit wait for the hope of righteousness by faith." We are waiting for, we are expecting righteousness—inward, proper, true ways of obeying God. We are expecting this to take place in us by the indwelling Holy Spirit of God, the Lord Jesus Christ working His will in us. This will happen through the Holy Spirit in us because we believe in God. This is an inward thing in your personal relationship with God, not an outward thing.

30

NOT OUTWARD ACTION, BUT INNER ATTITUDE
(5:6)

Have you ever considered the fact that outward action does not count as much as inward intention?

Being a Christian is a matter of the heart and of heartfelt conviction. The depth of a person's faith in God is not apparent on the outside. That is something in his own soul. Salvation is gained by yielding oneself totally to Christ Jesus and not by one's outward actions and the keeping of regulations. Paul insisted that living by faith in Christ Jesus is different than the world would think. Only the person who lives a yielded life can understand.

"For in Jesus Christ neither circumcision availeth any thing, nor uncircumcision; but faith which worketh by love" (5:6). If a person is living in Jesus Christ, he is a Christian. Outward actions are not primarily significant. The meaning of what Paul has written will become clear if the reader will insert here the word *baptism*: "Neither baptism availeth anything or being unbaptized." This would be true for any mode of baptism. The apostle is saying, if a person is living in Jesus Christ, it does not make a great deal of difference whether he has been baptized with water or he has not been baptized with water; it is faith that counts. This is not meant to belittle baptism or circumcision. What matters is the inward reality. The outward action does not count. This whole truth is a good deal like being married. Whether there is a wedding ring or not does not make any difference. A wedding ring does not add nor take away. What really counts is the love and affection that is between the husband and the wife.

This is what the apostle is saying here. When he writes "in Jesus Christ" he is again emphasizing that when the believer is living his life, he is letting God live His life in his heart. That means the believer has committed himself to Christ and has received Him into his life. Jesus of Nazareth taught:

> Abide in me, and I in you. As the branch cannot bear fruit of itself, except it abide in the vine; no more can ye, except ye abide in me. I am the vine, ye are the branches: He that abideth in me, and I in him, the same bringeth forth much fruit: for without me ye can do nothing.—John 15:4-5

This is part of the inward truth of being a Christian that only a Christian can fully understand. And this is the truth that is in Christ Jesus. This means living in a personal relationship with God in such a way that the believer is trusting in Him, yielding to Him. Then God is working in him "to will and to do of his good pleasure." God living His life in the human form of the believer is the truth "as it is in Jesus."

So far as the name "Christ" is concerned, this means that the believer is living his life yielded to and joined with Jesus Christ so that he has God the Holy Spirit operative in him. This is Christian living, not going by outward appearance, but by an inward relationship. The believer is depending on God and He is working in him. Now for the person who is thus related to God, in Jesus Christ, trusting in God, yielding to God, having the Holy Spirit working in him, circumcision doesn't matter and water baptism doesn't matter. The outward ceremony of circumcision, while it indicates the inward truth, does not add anything to the worshiper. It is not determinative. It may be indicative; it may indicate something that is important, as important as a wedding ring. The outward sign is important, but it cannot change anything. What really does change things is "faith working by love."

Faith—this alone is significant; the heartfelt response in participation in the will of God. The Christian has faith when he understands what God wants, and yields himself to let Him do it through him. The Christian's heartfelt response to the will of God leads him to accept the promises of God, which are "yea and amen in Christ Jesus." Faith shows up as a matter of obedience. When the believer obeys, it is a matter of obedience to His inner guidance. When a person believes in the Lord Jesus Christ, he receives Him as his Savior. He looks on God as his Father. He is trusting in Him and yielding to Him. The truth is that He comes to dwell in the believer, by the function of the Holy Spirit. When the Holy Spirit is thus operative in the believer, the believer is inwardly led by the Spirit of God, this is faith; and this is the faith that actually makes the difference. This involves the believer in the situation: "faith which worketh by love."

This would also be love toward God. The believer is being moved by an inward desire to do the will of God. "We love him if we keep his commandments." If a Christian has the disposition to do His will, this inward response to Almighty God works in him to move him to want to do God's will. This means love toward God and toward his fellow man, seeking his welfare and his benefit. Actually the Christian will expend himself on behalf of other people. This is the way in which love works out. Response to God will take the form of a person wanting to do His will and wanting to help other people. What makes all the difference is the heartfelt obedience and response to the inward guidance of the Holy Spirit of God.

31

OBEDIENCE
CAN BE HINDERED
(5:7-10)

Do you think it is good to have contrary ideas set forth?

Being a Christian is a matter of how a person thinks in his heart. In this connection a very sobering truth is that it is possible for a person to hold ideas in his heart that will prevent him from ever becoming a Christian. To become a Christian is to arrive at a certain place of inward conviction. "As a man thinketh in his heart, so is he." It is a man's personal understanding of God, of Jesus Christ, and his yielding himself to Him. All of this is an inward matter.

Suppose a person has the idea there is no God. Such a person could never believe in Christ, because Christ is the Son of God. If there is no God, then there is no Son of God. Again suppose someone took the position, "I just don't believe in miracles. Miracles are impossible." Could he believe the New Testament, the Bible, or the Lord Jesus Christ? Why, no! In becoming a Christian it is necessary for one to believe in the resurrection of the dead. If a person cannot believe in any miracle he cannot believe in the resurrection. Someone else may say, "I don't believe in hell." Then there would be no point in having a Savior. It would mean no one is lost. Another might say: "I don't believe in any judgment. I don't think God would judge anything. I don't think He would destroy anything." If God would not judge and God would not destroy, there is no need of a Savior. Thus it becomes obvious it is certainly possible to have ideas in the mind which are of such a nature that they prevent any chance of a person becoming a Christian.

It is also possible for a believer to get ideas that will hinder his spiritual growth. This had happened among the Christians in Galatia. Paul had led these people from paganism to Christian faith, and had founded these churches. Now other men had started preaching their own ideas among the Christians. Paul points out that obedience to God can be hindered in Christians by ideas which they hear. It is always dangerous when one is seeking to have people understand the gospel to have someone else come along and teach them differently.

"Ye did run well; who did hinder you that ye should not obey the truth?" (5:7). They made a good start. Why were they not growing as Christians? This is always a relevant question to ask anyone. There are those who have accepted Christ, perhaps even joined the church. They have taken the first step; but as the years go by, they never grow. Is it possible that one of the things that hinders them is preachers who do not preach the truth? Is it because there are men who stand in the pulpit and talk about everything else except the Lord Jesus Christ? Or is it possible they have been hindered by teachers in Sunday school who do not present the gospel? — HINDERANCES —

Could it be there are churches who do not care? Churches who do not pray? Is the reason why some people do not grow in the Christian life because there are critics in the church that are tolerated? Are there members of the congregation who question the Bible? Is this what hinders people? Are there professed believers who condone all kinds of questionable conduct, who do every worldly thing? These are sobering possibilities. There may be real reasons why some young Christians do not grow in faith and knowledge.

"This persuasion cometh not of him that calleth you" (5:8). The things that hindered these young Christians did not come from the preaching that had won them to faith.

"A little leaven leaveneth the whole lump" (5:9). This is a repeated statement in the Bible. It would not take many tainted ingredients to spoil the batter. Just one rotten egg would spoil the whole cake. It does not take much poison to kill. This is all a very serious business, and that is what Paul is warning about here.

It is very disconcerting to realize how easily the bland impression is given that anything goes in this free country. In the church particularly there seems to be a very sharp disposition to criticize anyone who is skeptical about new ideas or wishes to have proof for what is said. The people apparently are supposed to shut their mouths and listen. They are expected to open their ears and let anyone say anything he wishes. Instead of Bible study, groups are organized to have consultation and to gather around in "buzz" sessions. Our leaders seem to not want a real Bible teacher, but seem to think it better to let everyone talk. If someone talks who does not believe, someone else will say, "He has a right to his opinion." And though it may be true he may have a right to his own opinion as a public citizen, should this give him the right to set forth his own opinion inside the church? Here it needs to be remembered: "A little leaven leaveneth the whole lump."

"I have confidence in you through the Lord, that ye will be none otherwise minded: but he that troubleth you shall bear his judgment, whosoever he be" (5:10). Paul was confident that the Galatians would remain steadfast. Did he think they were of better stuff than other people, and so less liable to error? It may be that Paul had confidence in what he had taught them. Perhaps Paul had hope that having once tasted the truth, they would remember it. But he is sure that God will judge those who were responsible for the paralyzing confusion that existed in Galatia.

This would apply in similar situations today. The truth is that the Christian lives by faith. "Faith cometh by hearing," and hearing depends on the teaching and preaching of the Word of God. Therefore, if the teaching and preaching are unsound, bringing in things that are not true, faith will be weak. Great harm can be done by teaching error.

32

FAITHFUL PREACHING
AROUSES HOSTILITY
(5:11-12)

Do you know there is bitter hostility against any preacher who will insist on preaching the Bible without compromise?

The Christian gospel provokes resentment when it is preached in a straightforward manner. There is something about it that offends some people. I remember one time when I was preaching in a city in West Virginia. In order to make my message clear, I presented the idea to them that people would be saved only through faith in Jesus Christ. I indicated that "there is none other name under heaven given among men, whereby we must be saved" (Acts 4:12). The next morning I received a bitter note from a local lady. She called me arrogant, proud, hard hearted, and conceited. In her protest she complained: "You claim there is no other way of being saved than just your way." That was the way she put it. She seemed to miss the point that I was only faithfully presenting what the Bible teaches (John 14:6).

There is an exclusive note in the gospel that will provoke hostility on the part of some people. The Lord Jesus said, "I am the door: by me if any man enter in, he shall be saved" (John 10:9). He also taught that if anybody comes in by any other way, he is "a thief and a robber." "Neither knoweth any man the Father, save the Son, and he to whomsoever the Son will reveal him" (Matt. 11:27).

Peter said on the Day of Pentecost, "Therefore let all the house of Israel know assuredly, that God hath made that same Jesus, whom ye have crucified, both Lord and Christ" (Acts 2:36). Later he went on to say that "there is none other name under heaven given among men, whereby we must be saved" (Acts 4:12).

This truth still disturbs many people. And there are other things that make people angry. Some people are shocked when they hear the phrase "total depravity." To them that sounds awful in human ears. Yet this is just another way of saying: "You must be born again," and "flesh and blood shall not enter the kingdom of God." This is to say that men are altogether lost, apart from Jesus Christ. There is only one Son of God and there is only one way of salvation. It is the "way of the cross" that leads home. This is not being proud or arrogant, God forbid; this is just being truthful.

Anyone reading the Bible knows that it tells the story of the virgin birth. Yet many times people say: "Well, that's one view." If one points out that it is recorded in Matthew, some will say, "Oh, that was Matthew's theory." Then again it will be said, "That's Luke's theory," as if there were other valid ways of seeing it. At this point one can be amazed at the power of nonverbal communication. A great deal can be conveyed with a nudge in the ribs, a raised eyebrow, a wink. Such hints may convey a message, but can they communicate a message that will save the soul? Such procedure would bypass the Word of God.

The apostle Paul recognized hostile opposition. He did not hesitate to admit to the Galatians that this was due to his message. "And I, brethren, if I yet preach circumcision, why do I yet suffer persecution? then is the offense of the cross ceased. I would they were even cut off which trouble you" (5:11-12).

Apparently some people claimed that Paul allowed the use of circumcision as a religious practice to promote spiritual growth, as though he admitted there was some value to observing ceremonial rules. From what is recorded in the Book of Acts such an interpretation could be placed on Paul's conduct, because he had on occasion allowed the ceremony in deference to the people who practiced it. On one occasion he actually practiced circumcision, as in the case of Timothy, since his mother was a Jewess. Yet on the other hand, he refused to let Titus be circumcised, because Titus was a Greek. And so Paul argues, "If I in my teaching actually allowed that the use of ceremonial practices could be permissible, why do they persecute me?" He was obnoxious to these very people because he refused to concede any spiritual value in outward compliance or performance of regulation.

In other words, if today it would be said there is some value in human effort, so that there would be such a thing as being a Christian apart from self-denial and self-crucifixion, then the true gospel message would not be held to be so objectionable. Then it might be understood that a person could become a Christian by just improving himself a little bit. In that case people would not object so much.

If a teacher says plainly, "You must be born again," some will ask, "Why?" The answer of course is that no man is good enough. Some do not like to hear this. The statement "You must be born again" is a threat to every smug, self-satisfied, complacent person. Such opposition takes the form today of preventing the Word from being heard in strategic places. Some big meeting may be planned and men will hunt around to find a preacher. Perhaps there is a man who can actually preach a powerful message. He has the gospel in his heart, he has the flow of language, he has the right voice for it; and he could give them a wonderful message. But this man will tell them that they must be born again. He will tell them that they need to be saved by the grace of God in Christ Jesus. He will insist that the Bible message is the truth. It is a sad fact there may be several people on the committee who will say, "We cannot use him. He is too narrow minded." Then the committee will say, "We must find somebody else who is more acceptable." Paul's reaction to that kind of opposition was to deny its validity.

PART EIGHT

THE LAW OF
LOVE AND SERVICE

(5:13-18)

33

LIBERTY
IS FOR SERVICE
(5:13-15)

Do you realize a person could use liberty to his own hurt?

Christian life provides great liberty to the person who is being saved. It is wonderful when a man is free from the law. When one is no longer under any specific rule, when one does not have to watch regulations or be subject to restrictions, there is a wonderful freedom. But in this liberty there is a danger. When a man's debts have been canceled so that he does not owe anything any more, there is always the possibility for that man to make more debts. Parents find this to be true. Their child may have fallen behind with his work, and the parents may come along to help him. So the result is that the parents actually do the child's work. Then it may happen that if the child has not been well trained, he may actually fall behind again.

This can happen in the case of a young Christian. For example, a young man reared in a Christian home with family prayers and Bible reading every day, attending church and Sunday school every Sunday, goes off to college. Now there are no more regulations as at home. No one will call him in the morning and get him started on his duties or ask him what he does in the evening. When Sunday mornings come, there is no one to make sure he will go to Sunday school or church. This young man will now be confronted with the temptation to abuse this liberty as license.

This is a common human tendency. Paul points out to the

Galatians that being in Christ delivers a man from rules. The Jewish people had set up rules and regulations by which they tried to satisfy the demands of the law. They had many regulations. They had to wash their hands in a certain way before they could eat. They ate their food in a certain way, and only certain kinds of foods might be eaten. There were certain days in the week when it was proper to do this and certain days when it was right to do that. Everything was carefully spelled out to make sure they would be right in the sight of God. Jesus of Nazareth had taught them, saying in effect: "That is not the way it is done. A man does not get right with God by keeping rules and regulations. A man gets right with God by looking into His face, trusting Him, yielding to obey Him." When a person becomes a Christian, he is delivered from all these rules; therefore he enjoys a great freedom. But there is a danger in this.

The apostle Paul taught that salvation is by faith and not by works. But now Paul warns the Christians that they should beware of a new danger that their freedom brings to them. This is the very danger that the young person will have when he gets away from home. This is the danger anybody has who gets to the place where he does not have to follow rules and regulations. The person who has been brought up under rules and is suddenly set free, is faced with a big temptation. He is tempted to use his liberty for his own pleasure.

> For, brethren, ye have been called unto liberty; only use not liberty for an occasion to the flesh, but by love serve one another. For all the law is fulfilled in one word, even in this; Thou shalt love thy neighbor as thyself. But if ye bite and devour one another, take heed that ye be not consumed one of another.—5:13-15

Christians have been set free; liberty is in the plan of God for believers. This is a freedom from rules and regulations, but this is not license to do as one pleases. This is actually freedom from regulations so that the believer may be ready to obey the guidance of God. Paul is warning that when the believer has freedom, when he has liberty from specific rules and regulations and is free to do as he sees fit, there is always a danger. It is true enough that the believer no longer has to keep rules and regulations; but it is not true that he is absolutely loose. Paul would say he was free from the law, but not from the law of Christ. Paul realized he was under the commandment of Christ by His Holy Spirit. He did not have to keep outward rules and regulations, but inwardly he was the bondslave of Christ.

Paul taught that the meaning of the law was that one should "love thy neighbor as thyself." Anything along this line is healthy. "For all the law is fulfilled in one word, even in this; Thou shalt love thy neighbor as thyself." Then he says in verse 15, "But if ye bite and devour one another, take heed that ye be not consumed one of another." But if Christians exercise their freedom in allowing themselves to show hostility to other people, they are in danger of destroying the whole fellowship. It is true that the believer can be expected to act like a mature person. It is true that he is personally responsible to the Lord Jesus Christ. The Christian stands open, free, and responsible to God. He is not loose; he cannot do as he pleases. Liberty is for service. The believer is free, but he is not free from God.

34

WALK
IN THE SPIRIT
(5:16)

Can you see that if you first did what was good you would never do what was bad?

Living in Christ is a great blessing. The believer is blessed in what he is saved from and blessed in what he is led into. Living in Christ leads to so many good and gracious things. One of the great blessings in Christ is that when a person is walking in the way of Christ, he is not walking in the way of evil. It is also true that what it leads into is good. But there is already a great benefit in what it leads away from. Living in Christ is not something that a person does because he is good or strong or wise. Living in Christ is something a person shares. Christ is real! He is a Person! And living in Him means the believer is not alone. Living in Christ is having a fellowship with Him in which the believer participates. Living in Christ, participating in personal fellowship with the Lord Jesus Christ, is not only a great blessing because of what the believer receives from Him, but it is a great blessing in what it saves the believer from.

Consider this. If a person had a vacant lot, what could be expected to grow on that vacant lot naturally without any attention? There would be only weeds! It would be an unsightly affair. But if that person was to put in a garden there, cultivating and planting it, there would be vegetables. Or think of a person being responsible for the care of a group of boys. If that person was to turn that group of boys loose, and they were to spend two, three, or four hours together in some place, there could be trouble. On the other hand, those boys could have a wonderful time playing baseball, if someone was channeling their energies into a constructive program. This is what Paul means when he writes: "This I say then, Walk in the Spirit, and ye shall not fulfil the lust of the flesh" (5:16).

Later Paul draws attention to wonderful blessings that come as a believer walks in the Spirit. But just now he underscores a certain negative truth when he is saying that if a person walks in the Spirit, he will not fulfil the lust of the flesh. Paul is insisting all the way through that it is far more important to walk with the Lord than to obey rules and regulations. In other words, if a person was to go to church, that is good. But if he went to church twice on Sunday that would be good. Regardless of how often he went, if he did not have personal fellowship with the Lord Jesus Christ he would not grow spiritually. Just going to church will not promote your spiritual life; just singing in the choir will not promote your spiritual life; even giving money to missions will not promote your spiritual life as such.

Paul insists a person needs to have personal fellowship with the Lord. A person needs to know Him and to walk with Him. Naturally, if a person was in personal fellowship with the Lord Jesus Christ, he would go to church, give to missions, and pray. In fellowship with Him, a person would grow. Being in personal fellowship with the Lord Jesus Christ means walking in the Spirit. Paul urges believers to "walk in the Spirit." They should live their lives as guided and energized by the Holy Spirit. The Holy Spirit would take the things of the Lord Jesus Christ and show them unto the believers. In the last analysis, the real, dynamic factor would be "Christ in you," the hope of glory. God gives the Holy Spirit to all believers. But the believers must receive Him. They must know, appreciate, esteem, and honor the Holy Spirit. God sends Him and believers receive Him. Before one can have the Spirit, before God will send Him into the heart, a man must be a believer. He must know that Christ Jesus died for his sins, that Christ Jesus actually offered Himself as a reconciliation of the man to God, that Christ Jesus had done what was necessary to effect the atonement of bringing a man into the presence of God. This is basic if one is going to walk in the Spirit.

The truth could be summarized in this way. When a person knows he is a sinner, he knows he is lost and condemned. When this person, a lost and condemned sinner, hears and believes that Christ Jesus died for his sin, he understands that because he believes in Christ Jesus, God forgave him. He knows he is forgiven, and he is grateful for that. He knows that because Jesus Christ rose from the dead, he also can rise from the dead; and a new life is possible. He understands that Jesus Christ went to the cross willingly. By faith, he goes with Him, denies himself, is crucified with Christ. And just as God raised up Jesus Christ from the dead, the believer experiences in himself that he is raised in the newness of life. The believer knows that the living Lord sent forth His Holy Spirit into the hearts of believers to show them the things of Christ. The believer ingrateful obedience will yield himself to obey the will of the living, indwelling Lord Jesus Christ, the living God. Such a person walking in the Spirit, affected by the personal presence of the Lord Jesus Christ, will not fulfil the desires of the flesh. The believer may have promptings of appetite, passion, or vanity, but he will not fulfil them if he "walks in the Spirit."

35

DELIVERANCE IS
GUARANTEED IN OBEDIENCE
(5:17)

Do you realize that no Christian while living in this world can ever be one hundred percent in favor of what he is doing?

To be a Christian involves unending conflict within one's own soul. No matter how strong a man's faith may be, there is always the dead weight of his own human nature. Every Christian has two natures in him. Paul calls one of these the old man, and the other he speaks of as the new man. Paul refers to the first as the flesh, and to the second as the Spirit. When Paul uses the word "flesh" he means all that a person has in himself from his parents, his community, his country. All that a man has from his human birth and from his natural life is included in flesh. Many times the word *flesh* is used as if it were something bad or immoral. But flesh does not necessarily mean bad, or as bad as it could be. There can be good flesh and bad flesh. The word *flesh* as Paul used it includes all of civilization—culture, refinement, art, and music.

By the word *Spirit* Paul refers to everything a person has from his new birth, when he was born again, when he was regenerated—everything that he has from God through Jesus Christ. In the flesh a person is inclined to act in one way; in the Spirit he is inclined to act in a different way. It is this which causes tension. In order to reduce the tension in a person's heart, in this conflict within the Christian's experience, Paul would urge the believer to "mortify the flesh" and to feed the Spirit, to reckon the flesh to be dead and to nurture the things of the Spirit.

"For the flesh lusteth against the Spirit, and the Spirit against the flesh: and these are contrary the one to the other: so that ye cannot do the things that ye would" (5:17). By "flesh" Paul means all that a person has as a human being. Some of this a person may be conscious of; much of it he is not. The flesh has its own interests and its own desires, and it contends against the Spirit. By "Spirit" Paul means everything the believer has in Christ. The believer has much blessing in the Lord Jesus Christ of which he is not even aware, but it belongs to him because he belongs to Christ. Just as the word *flesh* means everything a person receives through the senses—what he hears, what he sees, what he smells, what he tastes, what he touches—so the word *Spirit* means everything a person receives through faith, because he receives these things from God by faith.

This conflict between the flesh and the Spirit need not be divisive in the personality. It will create some strain, but it does not have to split the person. This conflict inside the believer can be resolved. The believer can vote against the flesh. He can mortify the flesh. He can vote for the Spirit. The Christian can encourage and nurture the Spirit. Then the Spirit will become stronger, while the flesh will become weaker. When the believer has the Spirit stronger and the flesh weaker, he will not be in so much trouble; for the Spirit will control the flesh.

To have one of these two in control brings peace. Toleration of both will mean trouble. The believer cannot keep both in his heart at the same time. If a person is controlled by the flesh, Paul, writing in the Book of Romans, would call him carnally minded. If he is letting the Spirit rule, Paul would call him spiritually minded. Insofar as believers are concerned, they still have the flesh with them. As long as believers are in this world, they have the flesh. And as long as the flesh is still alive, there will be some inner frustration. As Paul said: "Ye cannot do the things that ye would." On the one hand, the Spirit that lives within the believer would like to move him to do the things of the will of God; but the flesh will not let him do it. On the other hand, so far as the Christian is concerned, he is never quite as selfish or as worldly as his flesh would like to be, because the Spirit will restrain him. In fact, if he is primarily interested in serving the Lord, he will devote himself to prayer and to a study of His Word. He will devote his money to the service of the Lord and will seek to follow along that way.

36

VICTORY IS POSSIBLE
(5:18)

Do you know how a Christian can arrange to win all the time?

Christian living involves unending conflict between the flesh and Spirit. The human nature is never satisfied with the way things are. It always wants things a little better and a little easier. But the Christian can thank the Lord because there is in him also another nature: God by His mercy has put in him the grace of the Lord Jesus Christ. The believer finds in himself a disposition to want to do the will of God. He would love to be well pleasing in the sight of God. He finds a joy in the favor of God. And yet the conflict goes on. By way of illustration anyone that has any money in the bank has won a victory. He could have spent it. Since that money is in the bank, it means that he overcame the tendency to spend it; he put it away. When an honest person tells the truth, it is a victory. He has resisted the temptation to lie and to deceive. He could have been careless in what he said, but he told the truth. Just so, when anyone is good, in any sense of the word, his virtue is an achievement; for vice is easy. Vice is like water running down hill.

"But if ye be led of the Spirit, ye are not under the law" (5:18). If a person is led of the Spirit, he is in the clear. There are definite prerequisites to being led by the Spirit. If one is going to be led by the Spirit, he will have to repent and turn to God. There must be faith: a calling on the name of God in Christ, with the acceptance of Jesus Christ. The Holy Spirit will not work in someone who does not belong to the Lord Jesus Christ. The believer must accept Him and receive His Holy Spirit. When a person is led by the Spirit, he is conscious that it is the Holy Spirit who is leading him. There will be deliberate obedience in response to His guidance. The believer must make up his mind to walk with Him.

If the believer does these things he will not be "under the law."

Being under the law means doing things in the natural way. This is where the person was born as a human being. In nature, the law of the harvest will prevail: "Whatsoever a man soweth, that shall he also reap." All men naturally are there. Under the law, a person will get what he deserves. The natural process works itself out, and that means that all will work out in sin, because there is not any man that has not sinned. And this will work out to his doom.

Praise His Name, the believer need not live in his own nature. He is called of Christ to commit himself to God. Every single believer has the opportunity of walking with the Lord. In this way a Christian can arrange to win all the time. He can receive the Holy Spirit of God, yield himself to the Holy Spirit, look into the face of the Lord Jesus Christ, remember the things of the Lord, and yield himself to Christ. God in grace and mercy will bless him and he will find that it is wonderful!

PART NINE

THE WORKS OF
THE NATURAL MAN

(5:19-21)

37

THE WORKS
OF THE FLESH
(5:19-21)

Do you realize that just doing what comes naturally will keep you out of heaven?

Christian living features the continual victory of the Spirit over the unending, everlasting way of the natural. It is the Lord Jesus Christ who makes the difference. The believer is not good enough or wise enough. His victory is that Christ lives in him. In Galatians 5:19-21 Paul comes to grips with the problem of Christian living. The issue is simply that the human being has a nature of his own, and the Lord Jesus Christ came to save him from that. Christ comes to "deliver us from this present evil world," and this has its connection with the believer through his human flesh. The procedure by which Almighty God through the Lord Jesus Christ will "deliver us from this present evil world," from our human flesh, is by the way of reckoning our human flesh dead, that Christians might be alive unto God.

> Now the works of the flesh are manifest, which are these; Adultery, fornication, uncleanness, lasciviousness, idolatry, witchcraft, hatred, variance, emulations, wrath, strife, seditions, heresies, envyings, murders, drunkenness, revellings, and such like: of the which I tell you before, as I have also told you in time past, that they which do such things shall not inherit the kingdom of God.—5:19-21

Not every person shows all these human traits. However, the phrase "such like" is just elastic enough to stretch out over most anything any person would do naturally. Anyone seeking to walk with the Lord knows these things are wrong. Some will need to take a second look at "idolatry." Many may feel this refers to idol worship of some pagan sort. Truly, they may have their idol worship, as did the Greeks and the Romans. But that is not what Paul means. What is idol worship for a Christian? Anything else other than God. Anything that has the heart's attention and will gain personal preference over God. Anything to which a person gives first place: money, one's job, personal prestige, appearance, one's family. It does not have to be crude. Another practice listed is "witchcraft." No doubt whatever was going on in the days of Paul is still going on in the world today. "Hatred" is well known and is a work of the flesh. "Variance" means being quarrelsome, taking the opposite view. "Emulation" is the effort to "keep up with the Joneses." There are people who will want to do that, but that too is of the flesh.

In this catalogue are listed activities that are vulgar, refined, personal, and secret—all intermingled, and all obviously unacceptable. They that practice such things are living in the flesh. Such people "shall not inherit the kingdom of God." When Paul speaks of the kingdom of God he means being yielded to God. "For the kingdom of God is not meat and drink; but righteousness, and peace, and joy in the Holy Ghost" (Rom. 14:17). The kingdom of God is something wonderful to be received by believers. The natural things a person does to please himself will not bring him into the blessing of God. The works of the flesh are not the way in which a person can receive the blessing of God.

PART TEN

THE SPIRIT FILLED LIFE

(5:22-26)

38

THE FRUIT
OF THE SPIRIT
(5:22-23)

Do you know that Christian conduct requires no effort?

Christian conduct, living and walking as a Christian, is not something one must work at to achieve. It is something that happens to the believer. Of course the believer makes arrangements about it, but it happens to him.

Consider a garden in which one actually produces vegetables. There is no doubt that much work is involved. And yet all the work is done with the soil. The gardener plants the seed and hoes the weeds. He fertilizes the ground, the plants, and irrigates the soil. But all that he was doing had nothing to do with actually making those plants grow. The gardener can be working all day and on into the evening. When he comes back the next morning or a few days later, he will find the plants have grown a great deal while he was gone. While he was asleep they were growing. It is their growing, the maturing, that really matters. God gives the increase.

This is the way it is with the Christian. And right here it is easy to make a mistake. Sometimes people feel the traits of virtue, charity, and goodness are produced by human effort in response to the praise of others. It is a common thing to flatter such persons, and this puts a big temptation before them. They get to thinking that they can do it. A person could get to feeling that if there is anything like peace in his soul, longsuffering in his spirit, gentleness in his manner, these things are his own doing. This would make him proud. He could become arrogant, and before he knows it he could actually be unbelieving. He would not be putting his trust in the Lord.

"But the fruit of the Spirit is <u>love</u>, <u>joy</u>, <u>peace</u>, <u>longsuffering</u>, <u>gentleness</u>, <u>goodness</u>, <u>faith</u>, meekness, temperance: against such there is no law" (5:22-23). The fruit of the Spirit is not the work of the believer. It is the work of Christ in his soul. When anyone finds a person to be unclean or hating or quarrelsome, that would be the old nature. But when one finds gentleness, goodness, faith, meekness in the Christian, it is not he that is doing it. That is being done in him and through him by the Lord Himself. It may be noted that the apple grows on the apple tree; the orchard owner does not have to do it. The Lord gives the increase: that fruit grows by the power of God.

By "love" is meant heartfelt concern in the welfare and happiness of other people. This is not the word in which a person is thinking of getting something. This is the word *love* according to the Bible, when one is thinking of giving something; and "the fruit of the Spirit is love." The soul can love God when it is interested in what pleases Him. A person can love his fellow man when he is interested in what pleases him.

"Joy" is an inner elation of spirit. It is when a person feels really good inside, even when he is in grief and has suffered loss; when the soul knows that the Lord is with him. A person can have joy in the midst of trouble, because he knows that the Lord is with him.

"Peace" is not merely the absence of quarreling or strife. It is instead an inner release from tension that comes from Christ Jesus. "Longsuffering" occurs when one continues on and on and does not stop even when he gets hurt. It is very closely associated with patience. "Gentleness" comes after longsuffering. Occasionally one sees a person with such good control of himself that even when he suffers all manner of indignity, he still remains gentle. Others will praise him and say, "Amazing! See how he had all that trouble, and look at how gentle he is." This can be done up to a certain point by will power. But when it is real "gentleness" it is more than human; it is from God through Christ. Gentleness comes after longsuffering.

"Goodness" is a matter of being helpful in one's influence and actions toward other people. There may be some people who are "good," but they are "good for nothing"! They are good in that they do not do anything wrong. But they do not do anything right either! True goodness will be in people who are good for you; they are good for the community. "Faith" as a fruit of the Spirit is beyond the faith by which one is saved. It means more faith than merely accepting Christ; it means actually having faith to live by—a faith one can put his weight on.

"Meekness" is only possible when a person is the victim of injustice. When someone does an injustice to another, then that victim can be meek. This means the injured person does not retaliate. A person may have every justification and opportunity to strike back, but he doesn't. A good word that could be used in place of "temperance" is self-control, or one could use "moderation." It can include total abstinence, but it is not necessarily so. It does not specifically mean dealing with alcohol, although it could. A person who is temperate is one who is controlled and moderate at all times.

"Against such there is no law." All this happens when the Holy Spirit in the heart is making the things of Christ active in the believer. The believer looks into the presence of God, into the face of the Lord Jesus Christ; he receives Him as his personal Savior and yields himself to Him. When the Christian will let Christ work in him, He will produce these things in him. The Christian need not strain, nor try, nor grit his teeth; he can relax, he can yield. He will find that these very traits are in him because of the presence of the Lord.

39

GETTING
A RIGHT START
(5:24-25)

Do you realize that living the Christian life begins with a definite start?

In Galatia Paul preached that salvation is the gift of God through Jesus Christ. If the Galatians believed in the Lord Jesus Christ, God would work in them "to will and to do of his good pleasure"; and He would set them free from this present evil world. All of this would be by the grace of God. It was free. If a man would just believe in the Lord, God would work it out in him and for him.

Others came after Paul and began to teach that Christians must keep certain rules. Believers should do the same as the Jews if they really wanted to grow in Christian experience. Paul knew that when a person gets to thinking he can do it, he will become proud and begin to depend on himself, instead of giving God the glory.

Paul made it clear that the same freedom which the Galatians had when they received the Lord Jesus Christ as their Savior is the very freedom that should be theirs when they live with Him as their Lord. It was true that the Lord Jesus Christ was the One who saved them; and He is the One who will direct them, because He is their Lord and Master. They came to the Lord Jesus Christ to be forgiven, and they live with the Lord Jesus Christ to be blessed and to be led. The faith they must exercise in this matter of walking with the Lord is the same kind of faith they had when they came to the Lord. In other words, the same attitude with which they were converted will be the one with which they can now be consecrated.

Paul argues that trying to keep the law is not an adequate way. He takes up the problem of living in the fullness of the life that Christ Jesus has provided. He deals with the matter of growing in grace and knowledge and coming to walk with the Lord: of becoming consecrated.

"And they that are Christ's have crucified the flesh with the affections and lusts. If we live in the Spirit, let us also walk in the Spirit" (5:24-25). Here are three stages of the truth. There is the first stage, "that they have crucified the flesh with the affections and lusts." Paul emphasizes that those who really belong to the Lord Jesus Christ are His, and this is wonderfully true. A Christian begins by crucifying the flesh. Then by daily living in the Spirit he goes on and walks in the Spirit. Christian living is not something a person drifts into. It does not rub off on a person. Becoming a Christian is based on a very definite decision. If one is going to be a Christian and live like a Christian, he must make a decision to die to self. In order to begin a marriage, there must be a wedding! So it is with the Christian life. There must be a stand for Christ, a definite commitment. Another example might be the matter of riding in a boat. Boat rides can be nice. But before a person can enjoy a boat ride, he must get into the boat. Right? Well, this is the way it is with becoming a Christian.

If one wants actually to live the Christian life, he must get started right. He must make a commitment to Christ. If one is going to walk with the Lord, there are some things he must leave behind. This is such a simple truth, and yet in Christian living it is sometimes missed. "They that are Christ's have crucified the flesh with the affections and lusts." And this attitude must be constantly renewed. A person does not do this just one time and then forget about it. Notice the strong word: he has "crucified" the flesh! That can be rough. It is not unfair to say that about this matter a person should be candid. A Christian should ask himself: "Have I crucified the flesh with the affections and lusts?" A great many believers never have any joy in their Christian experience and are weak as Christians because they did not get started right. Had they yielded themselves to the Lord and crucified the flesh with the affections and lusts, their relationship with Christ Jesus would have been different.

40

WALKING
IN THE SPIRIT
(5:25-26)

Do you realize that all a Christian need do for blessing is to just act the way he believes?

Christian living is really very simple for a believer. Paul puts it this way in writing to the Galatians: "If we live in the Spirit, let us also walk in the Spirit" (5:25). When Paul says "if," he does not imply doubt or suggest speculation. It could very well be translated, "Inasmuch as we live in the Spirit, let us also walk in the Spirit." Or, "Insofar as we live in the Spirit, let us also walk in the Spirit." Or Paul could have said, "Since we live in the Spirit, let us also walk in the Spirit." Paul used this same construction in language when he wrote, "If ye then be risen with Christ, seek those things which are above" (Col. 3:1). There was no doubt in Paul's mind that the Christians were risen with Christ, and this was his way of expressing a condition. Paul is exhorting the Galatians to live as they believe. He expects them to live first, in order that they should walk afterward. "Since we live in the Spirit, let us also walk in the Spirit." And how reasonable that is! It is a case of saying that you are *to be* before you are *to do*. And this is practical. If a person is right, he will do right. As Christians, they were right with God; now he is urging them to live that way. They were to live according to what they were, and whose they were.

Living in the Spirit means living from day to day as led by the Spirit of God. They had been moved to receive and trust the Lord Jesus Christ as their Savior, since they believed Jesus Christ had died and had been raised from the dead for them. They also believed that He had been taken up into heaven for them and that He was then interceding on their behalf. They believed that by His Holy Spirit He would guide them. Finally they expected Him to come again to receive them to Himself. Living in the Spirit means that they were maintaining themselves in the consciousness of these things. Remembering, believing, acting on these beliefs would be walking in the Spirit. Thus they would be moved to walk in obedience with the living Lord.

"Let us not be desirous of vain glory, provoking one another, envying one another" (5:26). This expression "vain glory" means they should not be too particular or sensitive about their reputation. "Vain glory" is the glory that makes a man vain—the kind of glory, or praise, that feeds vanity and makes one think he is someone big. After all, if a person is conscious of the things of the Lord Jesus Christ, he will remember that Christ Jesus died for him, that he was a sinner and under condemnation, and that if it had not been for the Lord Jesus Christ he would have been destroyed.

Some people seem to think that so far as God is concerned, anyone can come any time and in any way to make free with the things of God. It would be hard to imagine a more misleading impression than that. It is wonderfully true—anyone can come. The humblest, vilest—thieves, publicans, and harlots—can come; but they must come by God's way. The finest person in the country must come by God's way or he cannot come. God has a way. He showed it to us. The Lord Jesus said, "I am the way, the truth and the life: no man cometh unto the Father, but by me" (John 14:6).

It is true that without Him I am nothing. Yet He receives me. That should keep me humble. Now how foolish it would be for me to start building up a vainglorious reputation! If a person walked in the Spirit, he would live his life conscious of the Holy Spirit. And if he did that he would not be envious, or especially proud about the nice things people might say to him and about him. This would make other people jealous, and that would be such a hurtful thing in the Body of Christ. J. B. Phillips translates it this way: "Let us not be ambitious for our own reputation, for that only means making one another jealous." Oh, how much of the Lord's work is hampered by this!

PART ELEVEN

RULES FOR
NEW CREATURES

(6:1-12)

41

BEARING ONE
ANOTHER'S BURDENS
(6:1-2)

Do you know how Christians should act if one of them goes wrong?

Christian living should be featured by gracious kindness to those who are at fault. Every Christian has in him something of the old man as well as something of the new man that is in Christ Jesus. And that old man may trick him into sin. Sometimes Christians do fall into sin. That is obvious enough, but sometimes they fall into sin in subtle ways.

There was an occasion in the life of Noah when he became drunken, and he was lying in his tent uncovered. One of his sons, Ham, saw him and went out and told about it. Shem and Japheth took a garment, walked in backwards, and covered him. In due time Noah awoke; and when he understood what had happened, he pronounced judgment on this whole event. Noah pronounced blessing on Shem and Japheth for refusing to look on their father's nakedness. They would not take advantage of him in his trouble. They even covered him up so that he would not be seen. That action can be better understood when it is contrasted with that of Ham. When he saw his father in that embarrassing, unfortunate, perhaps disgraceful situation he went out and talked to others, drawing their attention. In so doing he disqualified himself from blessing. The curse received came not only on him, but also on his grandchildren. That is the danger of such misconduct: others may suffer because of it.

It is natural with human beings living together that when one of them breaks some custom, the others will turn on that one to destroy him. Human beings are ready to find fault! The destruction is not always a physical matter. Nor is it always an open, coarse, quarreling situation. The group does not always confront the wrongdoer. But there is one action the group can take, and that is to talk about that person. Some will pass the word around quickly, and it will spread far and wide.

All that is natural and it is of the flesh. That is not Christian, and Paul has something to say about it:

> Brethren, if a man be overtaken in a fault, ye which are spiritual, restore such an one in the spirit of meekness; considering thyself, lest thou also be tempted. Bear ye one another's burdens, and so fulfil the law of Christ.—6:1-2

Paul does not hesitate to point out to these Christians that they should be led of the Holy Spirit to have the same attitude toward that offending brother that the Lord Jesus Christ would have toward him. The Lord Jesus Christ would cover his sin.

The only person who ought to accuse him to point out his sin is Satan. Satan is the accuser of the brethren. Satan is the one who would gossip about him, but not the Lord Jesus Christ. In reading the New Testament, especially in the Gospels, there will not be found one instance when Jesus of Nazareth reported anything bad about anyone. Scripture says, "He knew what was in the heart of man." Jesus of Nazareth knew exactly what was in the hearts of people round about Him. He knew how mean they were. He knew how unclean they were. He knew how proud they were. But there is no record that He ever talked about it.

When Paul is saying, "You who are spiritual," he means, "You Christians who are being led by the Holy Spirit, who are conscious of the Lord and who want His blessing." Paul urges them to "restore such a one in the spirit of meekness." Put him back on the right track. "In a spirit of meekness"; that is, with no disposition to be personal about it; no feeling of superiority. "Considering thyself, lest thou also be tempted." One thing a spiritual Christian must be very careful about is to be oguard lest he fall in his own weakness.

Christians know perfectly well that in themselves they do not have any strength. Their strength comes from the Lord. This is true about every person. That being the case, one should have in mind that his human nature might break out at any time, and in his human nature he might do something that is improper. Since that is the way it is with each Christian, should not each understand how it could have happened with the other fellow? The Christian should forget about himself altogether; he should think in terms of the very best interest of the one who was taken in a fault. The first thing he should do with him when he is lying there naked is cover him up. If he is exposed in some disgraceful way, the Christian should not look at him. This will mean that if the Christian should be in a group of people who begin to gossip, he should not listen. Gossip will be to the other man's hurt. Since "love rejoiceth not in iniquity," the Christian will take no pleasure in hearing about any wrongdoing. By such gracious conduct, the Christian will be bearing the other's burdens. In this way he will be fulfilling the law of Christ.

42

FOOLING ONESELF
(6:3-6)

Do you realize how easy it is to make a fool of oneself?

Paul raises a question: Do you realize how easy it is for a man to make a fool of himself?

For if a man think himself to be something, when he is nothing, he deceiveth himself. But let every man prove his own work, and then shall he have rejoicing in himself alone, and not in another. For every man shall bear his own burden.—6:3-5

A Christian should be very careful in his opinion of himself. One of the common failings of man is to overestimate himself. When men fail in anything, they feel embarrassment because they fell short. If they have any kind of success, no matter how small it is, they gladly remember and report the success. So they build up about themselves a one-sided picture. It is then that a person could think something of himself, when he is nothing. How can a man avoid thinking of himself as something when he is really nothing? Paul indicates the answer: "Let every man prove his own work." If one were realistic and humble in his appraisal of himself and his actions, he would make a good start.

A person can be satisfied with his own actions without being vain or depending on someone else's opinion. If one keeps a close, accurate, candid, honest view of his own conduct; if he impersonally watches himself, and does not flatter himself, but admits the truth about what he is doing—then he will actually notice when he does something worthwhile. He will be rejoicing in his own estimate of what he has done and not in what somebody else says about what he has done.

Then the apostle Paul continues: "For every man shall bear his own burden." J. B. Phillips translates it, "Every man must shoulder his own pack." Some might want to use a phrase something like this: "Every tub must stand on its own bottom." Actually Paul is saying that if a person would be realistic and honest he would not need to depend on what other people say. Paul is warning against this peril of personal vanity, which is such a common danger even among good people. He directs that a Christian should be ready to help the other man along, if he stumbles. The believer should not indulge himself in the luxury of gossip. When the other man is in trouble, the Christian should keep it quiet, go to him, and help him out. And whatever he does, the Christian should have a realistic view of himself and not flatter himself. Christians should be willing to help each other, since they were helped when the Lord helped them. Paul continues by stressing that believers should live as Christians in obedience to the living Lord Jesus Christ. They can then rest assured that the Lord will bless them.

43

THE LAW
OF THE HARVEST
(6:7-8)

Do you think there is any way for a Christian to do wrong and get away with it?

Christian living brings results. The apostle Paul makes this clear in two of the most striking and most important verses in the whole Bible. They are a classic statement of truth:

> Be not deceived; God is not mocked: for whatsoever a man soweth, that shall he also reap. For he that soweth to his flesh shall of the flesh reap corruption; but he that soweth to the Spirit shall of the Spirit reap life everlasting.—6:7-8

This is the "Law of the Harvest." It states, so far as the whole universe is concerned, that God sees to it that things will remain consistent with themselves. Nobody living is going to plant oats and get wheat. "Be not deceived." Nobody needs to fool himself or let anybody else fool him; he need not be under any kind of illusion.

The gospel makes it clear to the sinner that he can come before God in his sins: "Though they be as scarlet, they shall be as white as snow." All his sins will be forgiven. God has cast all his sins behind His back. This is wonderful, but it is not a casual thing. All this is true for people who believe in the Lord Jesus Christ, but it should be kept in mind very clearly that it is not true for anybody else. When Jesus Christ steps in and takes sin on Himself so that He suffers for the believer, that is one thing. Results will certainly follow. But Paul warns against an easy error. "Be not deceived." At this point no one needs to be fooled. It is very seriously true: "God is not mocked." This is a way of saying very bluntly that God is no man's fool. Sometimes in the great desire to emphasize the goodness and the kindness of God, it is possible to exaggerate in giving a wrong impression. Some seem to say that because God is good, therefore anyone can come into the presence of God in any way: anything goes with God. This is not true! Anyone can come, if he comes by God's way. But He resists the proud. "Whatsoever a man soweth, that shall he also reap."

God's integrity guarantees that things will reproduce after their kind. This verse is the classic description in the whole Bible of the true meaning of the law. It amounts to this, that a person will get exactly what he deserves, exactly what he bargained for. At this point one should take a look at the deceitfulness of sin. Sin will suggest to the sinner that what he is about to do will not matter. That is not true. It will matter! When the suggestion comes to a person who is face to face with a temptation, "This doesn't look right but it will turn out all right," he is being misled. It will not turn out all right. Sin is sin, and this never varies. This is why Paul is so emphatic: "Be not deceived; God is not mocked: for whatsoever a man soweth, that shall he also reap." Should this make a person feel uneasy? Has he sown things that were not of the Lord? Is he about to reap them? The Bible makes it very plain that "he that sows to the wind shall reap the whirlwind." Results are going to come; this is as sure as anything can be.

"For he that soweth to his flesh shall of the flesh reap corruption; but he that soweth to the Spirit shall of the Spirit reap life everlasting" (6:8). This statement contains a sober warning—"he that soweth to the flesh shall of the flesh reap corruption"—and a gracious promise—"he that soweth to the Spirit shall of the Spirit reap life everlasting." This simply means that if in the course of living, and facing any particular issue at any particular time, the individual will act as his human nature suggests, doing the things that he likes to do, even though what he does may not necessarily seem so evil, yet "he shall of the flesh reap corruption." This will be the result for the one who is trusting in himself. "But he that soweth to the Spirit" is the person who in everything moves in the direction as led by the Holy Spirit, who will show him the things of the Lord Jesus Christ. "He that soweth to the Spirit shall of the Spirit reap life everlasting." When a person accepts Jesus Christ, the Spirit prompts him to yield to Him as his Lord. Now he wants Christ Jesus to control his activity, so that all he does will be subject to the will of the Lord. This person will reap "life everlasting."

The principle "Whatsoever a man soweth, that shall he also reap" is a wonderful call, with a wonderful promise. Believers can turn to the Lord, come to Him, put their trust in Him, yield to Him, and follow Him. Just as surely as that is true, the life of God will be in them and they will be blessed.

44

EVENTUAL VICTORY
(6:9)

What will help a man to keep on doing the will of God in the face of no results?

Christian living is a matter of acting in obedience to the will of God. Sometimes people get discouraged because they do not see immediate results. A person might do something because he thought it was right. He might make a sacrifice, but no one pays any attention to it. He might try to act the way he thinks the Lord wants him to act. He might work for the welfare of other people. He might do things for his own children, for his wife. And all the time he is compelled to realize that nobody seems to care about what he does one way or the other. This may be what the apostle Paul had in mind when he wrote: "And let us not be weary in well-doing: for in due season we shall reap, if we faint not" (6:9).

A person should be careful that he doesn't get the notion that he is going to reap all that he wants. He may be sure that he will reap something. "In due season we shall reap if we faint not." But the will of God sometimes leads into action that seems to have no promise in sight.

Walking in obedience to the will of God, and living in obedience to that will, may at times seem to be fruitless and pointless. Sometimes it can actually make the obedient ones a laughingstock, as well as objectionable, to other people. However, Christians do what they do because they feel in their hearts this is what the Lord wants them to do. After all, they are to be the salt of the earth. They are to be the light of the world. So when the light shows up the deficiencies and weaknesses in other people, what can be done? Must they hide their light? This does not seem proper. The only thing the Christian can do is to live his life and give his testimony. If he offends people, they will criticize him; they will object to him and abuse him. But what can he do about it? All he can do is to suffer; all he can do is to endure. When Paul wrote, "Let us not be weary in well-doing: for in due season we shall reap, if we faint not," he was encouraging Christians to expect desired results.

This matter of doing something that did not seem to make any sense was illustrated in the incident when Peter was in his boat, and the Lord told him to launch out into the deep and let down his nets for a draught of fishes. At first Peter told Him: "Lord, we were out all night fishing and we didn't catch any fish. There just aren't any fish out there." But faith in the Lord prompted him to add, "Nevertheless at thy word I will let down the net." Then he let down the net and caught so many fish he couldn't even hold them. No doubt, when Peter let down that net he felt like a fool. He knew there weren't any fish down there: he had been trying to catch them all night. But when he put down the net, this time there was more than he could hold.

Consider also the case of Martha on the occasion when Lazarus died. They had put him in the grave, and four days later Jesus of

Nazareth came. After He had met them and had talked with them, He asked: "Where did you lay him?" They took Him out and showed Him the grave. Then He said: "Take ye away the stone." Martha said at once, "Oh, no, Lord. He's been in there four days and his body is decaying by now. It would be very embarrassing for us to do this kind of thing." Jesus, however, insisted on it, reminding her, "Didn't I say to you that if you believed, you would see the glory of God?" He had them open up the grave and Lazarus came forth. Opening the grave seemed like a foolish thing to do, yet it was necessary in order that God could do His great work.

It is of special interest to note that when Peter let down the nets for fish, he felt like a fool; but he obeyed! When Martha took that stone away she felt it was a foolish thing to do, and yet she obeyed! A proper response to God in Christ Jesus would be, "Nevertheless . . . at Thy Word!" The believer will want to do His will. There may be nothing to indicate what can be expected when the person does what the Lord asks. Yet Paul gives the promise, "Let us not be weary in well-doing: for in due season we shall reap, if we faint not."

This "well-doing" will be a matter of obeying the Holy Spirit's guidance. There is no reference to works of mercy or to works of witness. "Let us not be weary in well-doing" means simply that, whatever it may be, the believer should not be weary of obeying the Holy Spirit. There is no promise here about winning souls. It may not be that at all. "They shall of the Spirit reap life everlasting." What a consequence, what a reward! Quite some years ago, when I was a very young Christian, my father-in-law knew that I expected to go to the foreign field, because I thought I was being called to go as a missionary. On one occasion he took me off by himself and asked me this question: "Why are you going to the foreign field?" And I remember in answering him, I tried to say, "I'm going over to win souls." Then he asked me this question: "Suppose nobody believes. Will it be a failure if you go?" I was stopped in my tracks. I remembered that I had tried to get the Lord to promise me that if I would serve Him I would win at least one soul, but He would not give me that promise. He gave me to understand, "If you want to serve Me, you will serve Me *regardless* of whether anyone comes or not." So when my father-in-law raised that question, "Suppose no one over there believes, will your going have been a failure?" I could not answer. He waited a bit and then said, "You may think you are going over there to help them change their ways. But suppose they don't want to change their ways; so they will not change their ways. Will your going then be a failure? Are you going over there to educate them and teach them how to live? Suppose they do not want to be educated and they will not change their ways of living. Will your going be a failure?" Then he went on to say: "Suppose you go over there and the first week you are there you contract a tropical fever and die within ten days. Would your going have been a failure?" By such questions he helped me to see that my going to the foreign field should not be primarily for the winning of souls. My going to the foreign field should not be to accomplish any particular record at all. My going to the foreign field should be an obedience to the Lord Jesus Christ—whatever the results might be. I was to go for the sake of Christ Jesus personally!

The Christian can be thinking in terms of his own home, shop, or office. Whatever his daily round of duty at home or in business may be, he can keep this in mind. He is to walk with the Lord and obey Him; then he will reap life everlasting. Whatever the results may be, He will watch over you!

45

HAVING LOVE
ONE TOWARD ANOTHER
(6:10)

How do you think a Christian should act in his neighborhood?

Christian life is primarily a matter of the believer's personal relationship with Christ Jesus. In the study of Galatians thus far, the importance of getting started right has been emphasized. "And they that are Christ's have crucified the flesh with the affections and lusts" (5:24). The believer accepts the call of the gospel and denies himself that he might walk with the Lord. A person can enter into this relationship in the privacy of his own soul at any given moment. The believer can yield himself to God. He can give up on himself, turn to God, and repent. He can admit that he is a sinner, accept Christ Jesus as his Savior and Lord, yield to Him as the Lord of his life, and he will receive the Holy Spirit. The Christian can do all these things right where he is. And these things are the very essence of becoming a Christian. No one else can possibly see from the outside what happens in the soul. Only God knows! Nor can any one else evaluate the believer's own personal responsibility to God. All this is done in the believer without showing any outward sign.

However, in Galatians 6:10 it is to be noted that expression of this new relationship is vital. While it is true that Christian life starts inside the soul, it is also true that for Christian life to be normal it must move outside: it must show itself. To grow into maturity as a Christian, which means to enter into and to cultivate consecration, until the person becomes thoroughly and really a consecrated Christian, he must bear fruit in the name of the Lord Jesus Christ to the glory of God. In order to do this, it will be necessary actually to live obediently in relationships with other people: to live in His will. The Christian may in his heart devote himself to the Lord, he may commit himself to Him, he may receive Him as his Lord and Savior, so that all this is actually real and true. Then this becomes operative, functional, produces results, and grows in itself as the believer acts outwardly in line with that inward commitment. Thus Christian life is eventually promoted by consistently serving other men.

Jesus of Nazareth said, "Thou shalt worship the Lord thy God, and him only shalt thou serve" (Matt. 4:10). Notice how those two words "worship" and "serve" go together. Worship is something done inside the heart as the believer responds to God. There may be certain means of worship, there may be certain outward things to do; but those outward things will not count unless the heart is actually considering and thinking about God. So while in his heart the believer worships God, it is also true that "Him only shalt thou serve." That would be in outward action. That would be with hands and feet!

This shows the twofold nature of the spiritual life, and the fashion of its occurrence. There cannot be any omission of either aspect. If the believer omits the worship, his service will not amount to anything. If he omits the service, his worship will not amount to anything. Each of these aspects must have its part, or both will shrivel and die. Both are needed. So first, the Christian will remember the first great commandment: "Thou shalt love the Lord thy God." This will mean worship. Second, he will remember the second great commandment: "Thou shalt love thy neighbor as thyself." This will mean service. The believer must have them both and in that order: first the worship and then the service. First a person gets right with God; then he serves his fellow man.

On occasion there is some confusion because people who have never accepted Christ are encouraged to serve. That is like telling a person who has never entered the water to swim. It is obvious that if one is going to swim, he must first get into the water. It is then that he can learn to swim. So it is with living the Christian life. First, a person becomes a Christian: accepts Christ. Then having accepted Christ, the believer serves.

It may help to picture the cross as one thinks of this truth. The cross has two beams: a vertical beam and a cross bar, a horizontal beam. Both are needed. If there is only the horizontal bar, it becomes merely a wooden beam lying on the ground. If there is only the vertical, it would be merely a post. There would not be a cross. To have the cross, there must be both the vertical that goes straight up to God, and the horizontal that goes to the people among whom one is living. In thinking of the cross, it is helpful to remember it is the vertical which points to God that holds the other one up. This indicates that the first thing is to get right with God; and then, second, be right with other men.

In this Galatian letter Paul spends much time in the early part clarifying the truth about the soul's response to God. There Paul emphasized that it is not by works, but by faith, that one receives the grace of God. In the Epistle to the Romans, Paul emphasized that a person is *justified* by faith. But here in this Epistle to the Galatians the emphasis is that a person is *sanctified* by faith. The same kind of faith exercised when the person believed in the Lord Jesus Christ and received Him as Savior is the very kind of faith exercised when the believer serves the Lord Jesus Christ and walks in Him.

"As we have therefore opportunity, let us do good unto all men, especially unto them who are of the household of faith" (6:10). Paul is saying that the Christian does not need to change his occupation. He may change it, but he does not need to do this; nor does he need to look for some particular program of service. Opportunities to serve will come. A Christian can accept his circumstances as being in the will of God. If he lives in a certain community, he can accept such opportunities given to him to serve in that place. If he has the grace of God in his heart in Christ Jesus, while he is in that community he will do good to all men, as he has opportunity.

The Christian may live in an area where there are some very poor people who are ill. Perhaps he can help by giving or serving in the local hospital. Perhaps he is in an area where there is an orphanage close at hand that can certainly use his help. In his congregation there may be a need for a Sunday school teacher. The Christian may think he is not much of a teacher; but if one is needed and he is willing to serve, this will be his opportunity to teach in Sunday school. The believer will not need to go out to make opportunities; they will come to him. The call will be presented to him.

The Christian will show himself as one of those who reverence God. He will honor God. He will participate in the public worship of God, and he will do good to all men by reminding them of the things of God. He will be the kind of person who gives thanks to God for the food he eats. He will respect and honor the Lord's Book, the Bible. He will respect His people, His church; and generally as he lives in his community he will be doing good to all men as he bears his witness to his personal reverence for God.

Also the Christian will show respect for authority. He will be the kind of person that keeps the rules and obeys the law. Because he is a Christian in his community, he will show regard for other people. Surely he will want his own liberty, but he will grant others their liberty. In his community there will be those who are poor. He will show charity toward those individuals. All such conduct is good; and thus he will "do good unto all men, especially those of the household of faith." The Christian will have a special interest in other Christians, to help them. All such conduct will enable the person to grow as a Christian.

46

RELIGIOUS PRACTICES CAN BE SUBSTITUTED FOR TRUE CHRISTIAN LIVING
(6:11-12)

Do you realize that prominent activity in church routines can be a substitute for true Christian living?

Christian living is essentially a matter of denying self in the crucifying of the flesh. "If any man will come after me, let him deny himself, and take up his cross, and follow me" (Matt. 16:24). "And whosoever doth not bear his cross, and come after me, cannot be my disciple" (Luke 14:27). Jesus of Nazareth demonstrated in Himself what this means. He willingly yielded Himself to be put to death on the cross in order that He could serve God and save us.

Christian living is like that. It is a matter of denying personal interests and yielding oneself to be reckoned dead in Christ, crucified with Christ, in order that the life of God in Christ might become operative in the believer. This means that the believer will give up on himself and on all his interests, in order that the will of God may be done in his life. This actually takes place in the soul without being seen on the outside. When a person yields to God, others find it out only afterwards; but the believer knows it in his own heart.

When the will of God actually functions in a person, the interests of human nature are clearly ignored. A Christian is not interested any longer in doing the things that other people are interested in doing. This can cause some hurt feelings. Once there was a young couple who experienced this. Each Saturday night this couple with several other couples gathered for a pleasant evening's entertainment. Their fellowship would last until quite late, so it was difficult for them to get their young children off to Sunday school the next morning. The day came when that young man and his wife saw that these Saturday night meetings were not helpful to them spiritually. They enjoyed their friends greatly, but these Saturday nights were spiritually destructive. So the husband suggested to his wife, "Let's have them all over to our place and we'll tell them how it is." They invited their friends and had one of their usual Saturday night meetings. Then this couple announced: "We are saying good-bye to these Saturday night meetings because from here on out we are going to make it a point to get our boy to Sunday school on time Sunday morning." This sort of thing will happen when Christians actually yield themselves to the will of God. It may break up certain human combinations, as it did in this case.

The cross of Christ means continual self-denial. It is the common lot of all who yield themselves to the Lord Jesus Christ to obey Him, that their human contacts will be changed. Because they are now doing things that are pleasing to God, they can expect to suffer persecution. There will be a good deal of pressure on any person not to live the Christian life. A person can go through the form of Christianity, observing the outward activities, without giving much offense. However, if he begins to do anything that will make a difference in his personal conduct, then he will feel the pressure. Because of this fact some will actually substitute participation in religious practices for personal self-denial. They will attend Sunday school regularly. It could be amusing if it were not so pathetic, to see how many there are who greatly appreciate the early Sunday morning service so they can go to church and get that over and done with, and then have the rest of the day to enjoy for themselves! Others feel they are good Christians all week long just because they went to church on Sunday. There are some who will say, "I know I am a good Christian. I don't dance, I don't drink, and I don't go to the theater." There need be no objection to any of this. It is possible that being delivered from many of those practices may actually be a good thing. But outward religious conduct can be a substitute for real, personal self-denial and deep-down, humble yielding to God. There are any number of people who get to be immoderately proud, just by thinking how good they are.

Paul warns the Galatians: "As many as desire to make a fair show in the flesh, they constrain you to be circumcised; only lest they should suffer persecution for the cross of Christ" (6:12). Some will urge the Christian to join in their observance of rules and regulations as a substitute for personal self-denial, feeling these outward practices can apparently satisfy all the demands of the gospel and Christian living. Actually deep down inside, such persons can be selfish, vain, proud, and self-indulgent. The apostle Paul would say that this is a great danger.

PART TWELVE

THE ABUNDANT LIFE

(6:13-18)

47

"IN THE CROSS OF
CHRIST I GLORY"
(6:13-14)

Do you know what a true Christian esteems above everything else?

For a Christian, the most wonderful thing in the world is the fact that Christ Jesus came to die for him. Everything else pales into insignificance before this tremendous fact, that the Son of God came to lay down His life for the salvation of this sinner. It is normal in a person's thinking to place different values on things and on various ideas and events. When a person puts God before everything else, then his heart and mind will be full of peace and joy. The natural man is inclined to esteem most valuable that which is his own. This comes naturally. It has been said that the sweetest sound in anybody's ear is that person's own name. To see one's name in print, to see pictures of one's own children, to hear about schools that one has attended is most interesting and this is very natural, very normal. Nor is there anything especially evil in this.

But this tendency can become a problem in spiritual living. It is possible to put something that is really lesser in first place. Even among church people, this disposition to esteem what is personal is apparent. In individual congregations, often unhappy conflict comes up between personalities, between Mr. Jones and his crowd and Mr. Smith and his crowd. Then the whole church is torn, and soon everyone is brought into the trouble between the Joneses and the Smiths. Many churches have had their programs and their spiritual lives actually paralyzed by contention and conflict between certain groups of people who are organized around certain individuals.

Paul warned the Galatians of the lengths some people would go to win other people to their personal causes. This happened at Antioch when the Jewish Christians came down from Jerusalem. They began to gather people who believed in Jewish customs. Even Peter and Barnabas joined them. Paul objected strenuously to anyone changing his ways for personal reasons, when the way of the Lord was open and plain for all to follow. Paul points out that often these very people who ask you to follow them are not able to carry out what they promise. "For neither they themselves who are circumcised keep the law; but desire to have you circumcised, that they may glory in your flesh" (6:13).

They actually want everybody else in the church to accept this ceremony of circumcision, that they may have a sense of importance because others joined with them. Paul expresses his own attitude by way of contrast. "But God forbid that I should glory, save in the cross of our Lord Jesus Christ, by whom the world is crucified unto me, and I unto the world" (6:14).

After he has asserted his own attitude in contrast to other teachers, he humbly points out that the crucial battle in the whole conflict between truth and falsehood, between light and darkness, between life and death is fought in the believer's own personal soul in his relationship with the Person of the Lord Jesus Christ. The whole essence of the Christian experience is, "What do you think of Jesus Christ? What will you do with Jesus Christ?" The question that Pilate asked in his dilemma is still the question that everyone must answer sooner or later: "What shall I do then with Jesus Christ?" It is as important as what is going to happen to the soul. In the last analysis it was the Christian's soul that was involved when Christ Jesus died for him. Everything is settled deep down inside the heart between the sinner and the Lord. Paul lays down this principle for all: "God forbid that I should glory." Paul would not put his confidence in anything, "save in the cross of our Lord Jesus Christ, by whom the world is crucified unto me and I unto the world." And that is the word that Paul was giving out anywhere, any time, any place.

48

A NEW CREATURE
(6:15-16)

Do you realize that the only thing that matters is that you should be born again?

Christian life is essentially a matter of being a new creature in Christ Jesus. That sentence should be taken with every word meaning exactly what it says. If a person wants to live as a Christian, he must by the grace of God become a new creature in Christ Jesus. He must be born again. This new birth is as significant and meaningful in life as the first birth was. The new birth in which a person is a new creature in Christ Jesus is not a new mode of himself. It is not his personality done over again. It is actually a new life in him. When I was born the first time, I was born of my father and my mother, as a human being. Actually the life in me was the life of Adam. That life was generated biologically. A person is a human being in the flesh because his father and mother begot him in the flesh.

When that person was born again, he was begotten of God, by His Word, His promises, and His Holy Spirit which he received. Therefore there was in him a new being. There is now in him an interest in doing the will of God. There will be around him a physical world he can hear, see, taste, touch, and smell. There is also for this new creature a spiritual world wherein one is conscious of God. While one cannot see God physically, or touch Him, He is very real. There is in the new man a capacity to be conscious of the reality of the invisible God. This invisible God is the creator. He is greater than the world He made. He is greater than any human being, and He is the One who judges all men. And before Him a person is responsible for the things that he does. Each man stands in the presence of God, and He deals with the man in his own heart. Almighty God is willing and able by His grace and power to impart Himself into the human heart as a new life. The believer is a new creation of God in Christ Jesus, so that he will be a child of God just the way he was the first time a child of man.

It is possible to attempt to look back to when one was born again and say, "I don't remember that happening to me." It may be true that one does not remember when he was born again, but neither does he remember the first time he was born. Yet it was real. There will be some who will remember when they accepted Christ. There will be some who will remember when they came to faith; and they may possibly say, "That's when I was born again." But one need not worry about whether he is aware or not aware when it all started. One can leave that with God. Jesus of Nazareth Himself taught: "The wind bloweth where it listeth, and thou hearest the sound thereof, but canst not tell whence it cometh, and whither it goeth: so is every one that is born of the Spirit" (John 3:8).

This is the background for Paul's comments to the Galatians: "For in Christ Jesus neither circumcision availeth any thing, nor uncircumcision, but a new creature" (6:15). What is necessary is the new creature. Whether a person is circumcised or not circumcised is a matter of the flesh. The real issue is a matter of faith. Does the person belong to the Lord? This cuts beneath all ceremony of any kind into the personal relationship with Jesus Christ.

"And as many as walk according to this rule, peace be on them, and mercy, and upon the Israel of God" (6:16). The matter of belonging to the Lord and being a Christian is not a matter of ceremony. What really matters is the life of God in you. Anyone who believes in the Lord Jesus Christ and has received Him as his Savior is a brother; and to such a person Paul would say, "Peace on him." He may not have been baptized the same way as others; but Paul prays: "Peace on him, and mercy upon the Israel of God."

49

BEYOND CONTROVERSY
(6:17-18)

Do you know how a person can be above all argument?

Christian life is grounded directly in the living Lord Jesus Christ. This is what makes a Christian. Jesus Christ came into this world to seek and to save the lost. He died for sinners. He was raised from the dead. He was taken up into heaven. He is right now at the right hand of God praying for them. And He will come again. All this is the work of God. "In the fulness of time God sent forth his Son." When one is dealing with the gospel of the Lord Jesus Christ he is dealing with the realities of Almighty God. All who have become Christians enter into a relationship with God in which they belong to Him. He is the Strong Tower. Believers can run into Him and be safe.

When a person receives Jesus Christ as his personal Savior, nothing any man can do will interfere with this. Mighty men of war cannot interfere with this. A man with a gun can shoot and kill the Christian, but he cannot interfere with the Christian's relationship with Almighty God. Others can beat the Christian and persecute him, but they cannot interfere with his relationship with Almighty God. This has been tried, all over the world. In all the past two thousand years, Christians have been persecuted. There have been all kinds of hurtful and vicious things done to them, but the fire has never been put out. The Christian belongs in the Lord, and God is Almighty. God is a Strong Tower and Refuge, and they are safe in Him. The apostle Paul had something of this in mind when he came to the end of his Letter to the Galatians.

"From henceforth let no man trouble me: for I bear in my body the marks of the Lord Jesus" (6:17). Paul was just one man, but he could talk for himself; and he could tell them plainly that Christ had put His hand on him. No one could change that. Paul personally belonged to Christ Jesus, and Christ personally belonged to him.

One time Jesus of Nazareth met a certain man who had been born blind. He dealt with him in such a way that the man was able to see. This healing was done on the Sabbath Day. The Pharisees first came to the man's parents and asked: "Who worked with this man, who did this?" The parents said, "We don't know. After all the young man is of age; ask him." So they asked him, "Who was the man that did this thing to you? Who is the man that opened your eyes?" He said, "I don't know; I don't know Him." And they said, "If you don't know Him, why would you let a thing like this happen?" The man said to them, "I don't know who He is or whether He is a good Man or not. Whether it was the right or wrong thing to do this on the Sabbath Day or not, I am not going to argue with you about that. But one thing I know: once I was blind, now I see." Before that kind of testimony all objections fall to the ground.

There is no kind of clever argument of any sort that can undo the testimony of a man who says, "I put my hand in the water and my finger was scalded." He knows that water was hot. There is a wonderful liberty and freedom and strength in personal relationship with the Lord Jesus Christ. "From henceforth let no man trouble me: for I bear in my body the marks of the Lord Jesus." Paul could say, "I bear in *my* body. I've had this thing happen to *me*, the marks of the Lord Jesus." The Christian life is grounded directly in the living Lord Jesus Christ.

Paul's Letter to the Galatians opened with sharp disagreement, because there were men in the church who were teaching unsound ideas. Paul argued that these new ideas so introduced were not really valid. In the latter part of the book he undertook to show the Galatians how they could grow and how they could serve in the Spirit. He urged them to live as they believed in the Lord Jesus Christ. Finally he brings forward the one consideration that actually certifies him to talk about this whole thing. "I bear in my body the marks of the Lord Jesus." He could say this because he had suffered enough for his testimony to be listened to and to be left alone. People had stoned him; undoubtedly there were scars. People had whipped him; there probably were welts on him. No doubt the body of Paul actually had the marks on it of what had been done to him because he was a believer in the Lord Jesus Christ. He had suffered for Christ's sake and he should be left alone. But there is probably a deeper meaning. Paul had personally crucified his own flesh. "I bear in my body the marks of the Lord Jesus" could mean he had personally denied himself. Paul actually experienced self-denial and self-crucifixion that he might win Christ.

"Brethren, the grace of our Lord Jesus Christ be with your spirit" (6:18). That is the one thing really needed. A person does not need the conclusion of a long argument. He does not need the judgment of a great many different considerations. What he needs for his spiritual experience, health, and strength is the grace of the living Lord Jesus Christ in his own soul. This grace will enable him to believe. This grace will enable him to understand. This grace will confirm him personally in his relationship with Christ, and this grace will strengthen him to keep him true and right in his attitude toward God.